GENESIS to REVELATION

1 AND 2
CORINTHIANS
GALATIANS
EPHESIANS

EDWARD P. BLAIR

GENESIS to REVELATION

1 AND 2 CORINTHIANS GALATIANS EPHESIANS

EDWARD P. BLAIR

PARTICIPANT

GENESIS TO REVELATION SERIES:
1 and 2 Corinthians
Galatians, Ephesians
PARTICIPANT

ISBN 9781501855214
Manufactured in the United States of America
18 19 20 21 22 23 24 25 26 27—10 9 8 7 6 5 4 3 2 1

ABINGDON PRESS
Nashville

TABLE OF CONTENTS

Whether Paul or Apollos or Cephas or the world or life or death or the present or the future—all are yours, you are of Christ, and Christ is of God. (3:21-23)

1
UNITY IN THE CHURCH
1 Corinthians 1–4; 16

> EDITOR'S NOTE: This study of the letters to the Corinthians, Galatians, and Ephesians does not run straight through the letters from beginning to end. In order to bring greater clarity to the material, Dr. Blair has chosen to deal with material from the end of several of the letters out of sequence and earlier in the study.

DIMENSION ONE:
WHAT DOES THE BIBLE SAY?

Answer these questions by reading 1 Corinthians 16

1. Where is Paul at the time of writing this letter, and what are his future plans? (16:1-11)

2. What does Paul desire the Corinthians to be and do until his arrival? (16:1-18)

Answer these questions by reading 1 Corinthians 1:1–2:5

3. What does Paul say about himself and about the church at Corinth in the opening greeting? (1:1-2)

4. What are the Corinthians quarreling about, and what is Paul's attitude toward their quarrel? (1:10-17)

5. Who are the advocates of the wisdom of the world? (1:18-20)

6. What is wrong with their attitudes and spirit? (1:18-23)

7. What is the result of their preoccupation with human wisdom? (1:21)

8. What attitude do the Christians have toward the preaching of a crucified Savior? (1:21, 29)

9. What results have come to them from believing in such a Savior? (1:18, 21, 24, 30)

10. Through what kind of words, concepts, and persons is the gospel properly proclaimed? (2:1-5)

Answer these questions by reading 1 Corinthians 2:6–3:23

11. By what terms does Paul describe the condition of the Corinthians? (3:1-4)

12. What three metaphors are used to explain who the Corinthians are in relation to God, Paul, and Apollos? (3:9, 16)

13. What ideas in 1 Corinthians 1–3 are summarized in 3:18-23?

Answer these questions by reading 1 Corinthians 4

14. Why is it wrong to judge others? (4:1-5; see also Matthew 7:1-5)

15. How do the attitudes of the Corinthians compare with the attitudes of the apostles? (4:8-13)

DIMENSION TWO: WHAT DOES THE BIBLE MEAN?

Paul's letter to the Romans is theology-centered. His letter to the Corinthians is life-centered or problem-centered. While we learn much from First Corinthians about the readers' beliefs, we learn more about their everyday life: at home, in the marketplace, and in the church. Everywhere we see tension between the church and the world, with problems for Christians, which are similar to our own. First Corinthians can help us in our struggles with the worldly attitudes and practices that threaten our Christian living.

The Acts of the Apostles (chapter 19) indicates that Paul spent more than two years at Ephesus on his third missionary journey. On his second journey, he founded the church at Corinth (Acts 18:1-18). Before long, serious troubles arose there, and news about them reached Paul in Ephesus.

The letter Paul previously wrote the Corinthians (1 Corinthians 5:9) apparently did not meet their needs and, moreover, was misunderstood (5:10-13). The sick Corinthian church urgently needed a doctor. Since the doctor could not come at the moment, he sent a lengthy prescription to them in the form of our First Corinthians. The letter probably was carried to Corinth by a three-man delegation (16:17).

■ **1 Corinthians 1:1-17.** Paul begins his letter, as was customary in his time, with a greeting (1:1-3) and a thanksgiving (1:4-9). In his letters, Paul regularly stresses his authority as a representative of God and Jesus Christ, often mentions one or more of his associates, includes descriptive words about the church to which he is writing, and enriches the traditional greeting by a reference to the peace (well-being) God and Christ give.

In the thanksgiving, Paul calls to mind his positive remembrances of the readers. He knows the power of praise to motivate progress in the Christian life. Even though the Corinthians have many serious faults, he still can find much to be thankful for: God's graciousness extended to them through their faith in Jesus Christ, their enrichment through God's gifts of speech and knowledge, and the clear evidence the Corinthians show of the validity of Paul's gospel and their ability to pass the test of God's judgment at the last day.

Paul plunges immediately into the Corinthians' most serious problems: quarreling and divisiveness in the church. The family of God and the body of Christ are being torn apart by wrangling and division into cliques. For Paul, the heart of Christianity is love: God's love for us, our love for God, and the family members' love for one another. "Do everything in love," he writes at the end of his letter (16:14). He knows that all the Corinthians' problems will disappear if love is both valued above all else and earnestly sought after (14:1).

The Corinthians are claiming superiority over one another by virtue of their attachment to different leaders: Paul, Apollos, Peter (*Cephas* is Aramaic for "rock"), and Christ (1:12). It is not clear whether there are four distinct groups, each with a theology supposedly patterned after the views of its leader, or whether individuals are simply being loyal to the person who baptized them into the faith.

Clearly, some people are making too much of baptism, apparently regarding it as a magical rite that ties the initiator and the initiated in an inseparable bond, such as one might enter into the mystery religions of Corinth. Though Paul approved of baptism (Romans 6:3-4; Colossians 2:12), for him it was effective only if one had deeply heard the gospel and responded to it in faith (1 Corinthians 1:13-17). Human leaders are not to be exalted to a place that belongs to Christ (1:13). And Christ and his people (Christ's body, 12:12-13) are not to be split up around these leaders. Only death to the body can ensue.

■ **1 Corinthians 1:18–2:5.** The divisive spirit rests on arrogant glorification of human wisdom (see 8:1-3). Human wisdom, particularly when eloquently presented, can empty the cross of Christ of its power to save (1:17).

The dispensers of human wisdom are "the wise man" (the philosopher), "the scholar" (especially the legal scholar), and "the philosopher of this age" (this world's clever arguer). Paul had jousted with them all and found them unreceptive, arrogant, and devoid of true knowledge of God (see Acts 17:16- 34). Human beings cannot speculate their way to God. Divine wisdom, set forth in simple preaching of the gospel, holds that God has come down to earth in Jesus Christ and his cross to save those who believe. The saved are often the unlearned, the weak, the lowly and despised—the nothings (1:26-28)—but they know in personal and group experience the life-giving power of God (1:3).

■ **1 Corinthians 2:6–3:23.** Though divine wisdom may appear foolish to the worldly wise, it is the highest form of wisdom to the really mature (2:6). "Mere infants" (3:1) will often prefer worthless tinsel to priceless diamonds.

Christian wisdom, which comes from God, not from humans, does not offend the mature mind. This wisdom is incarnate in Jesus Christ, "the Lord of glory" (2:8). Its purpose is the indescribable, external enrichment of believers (2:7-9). This wisdom, "God's wisdom, a mystery that has been hidden" (2:7) from human and demonic rulers, comes to believers through the revealing activity of the Holy Spirit, who dwells in them as God's gift (2:10-12). God's thoughts can be communicated only through words taught by the Holy Spirit to those who rely, not on human wisdom and human strength, but on divine wisdom and strength (2:13-16).

Human wisdom has set the followers of Paul, Apollos, and Peter over against one another. These leaders actually are fellow-laborers for God, not rivals encouraging partisanship (3:1-9). Each is accountable to God for the character of the work he does, not to other people (3:10-15). Their followers must not destroy the structure (the church) God's servants so laboriously and sacrificially built (3:16-17). When filled with God's wisdom, followers will see that God's representatives are not to be fought over but accepted in gratitude as God's means of enriching God's people (3:18-23).

■ **1 Corinthians 4.** Human judgment of God's messengers is presumptuous. God will see to their judgment at the proper time (4:1-5). Better than judgment is humble, sacrificial imitation of their life and spirit (4:6-13).

The Corinthians must take practical steps to overcome their foolish divisions: listening to their spiritual father; giving attention to Timothy's instructions when he comes; and preparing for Paul's impending visit so that they may meet in love and understanding (4:14-21).

DIMENSION THREE: WHAT DOES THE BIBLE MEAN TO ME?

1 Corinthians 16:5-9—There Are Many Adversaries

Paul was under great pressure and perhaps in deep suffering when he wrote this letter. The hostility of the Jews at Ephesus had led to his withdrawal from the synagogue (Acts 19:8-9). The silversmiths had hotly opposed his mission (Acts 19:23-41). He may even have been imprisoned there (2 Corinthians 1:8-10). At least, he came near death. Yet he wants to stay on, to enter the great door of service in Ephesus (1 Corinthians 16:9). Somehow he finds strength enough to wrestle with the many problems of the Corinthians in addition to his own.

What do you do when the going gets rough? Do you run away, or do you resolve to hold steady and enter the "great door for effective work" in your situation? Have you a source of power like Paul's (2 Corinthians 12:9-10)? Do you seek prayer support by God's people (2 Corinthians 1:11)? When should one run, as Paul sometimes does (Acts 17:10), and when should one stand firm?

1 Corinthians 1:10-17—Is Christ Divided?

The divisions in the church at Corinth rested on not only selfishness and cantankerousness but also basic theological misunderstandings: that Christianity consists in magical rites and ceremonies, such as baptism, and that its evangelists and teachers are special communicators of divine grace, to whom recipients are intimately attached.

Paul wants to tie the Corinthians to Christ, not to human leaders, and to point out that salvation comes by the response of faith to the Messiah who dies for us on the cross. Think about the church squabbles you have known. Analyze the causes. What part did selfishness and ambition play? What misunderstandings of the basic nature of Christianity on the part of the participants can you identify? What spirit did you show? What suggestions for improving your attitudes and the relationship of members have you gleaned from 1 Corinthians 1–4?

1 Corinthians 1:18–2:16-Divine and Human Wisdom

Intellectual people, particularly some philosophers, have been turned off by Paul's downgrading of human wisdom and his exaltation of a secret wisdom that is discerned only, or chiefly, by simple, uneducated, "spiritually minded" people. Intellectual people regard the cultivated human mind as the only doorway to truth, and Paul seems to deny sin.

Might Paul be right that the cultivated intellect cannot take us all the way to God and an understanding of life's ultimate mysteries? Must God come down to us, as in Jesus and in the Holy Spirit, as indwelling interpreter and guide? Try to work out your understanding of the relationship between divine revelation and human reason.

Do you not know that your bodies are temples of the Holy Spirit? . . . You are not your own; you were bought at a price. Therefore honor God with your bodies. (6:19-20)

PERSONAL MORALITY IN THE CHURCH

1 Corinthians 5–7

DIMENSION ONE: WHAT DOES THE BIBLE SAY?

Answer these questions by reading 1 Corinthians 5

1. What does Paul say about the nature and seriousness of the sin mentioned in 5:1?

2. What is the attitude of the members of the church toward the sin? (5:2, 6)

3. What are Paul's directions for handling the problem? (5:2-5)

4. What does Paul hope to achieve by handling the matter in this way? (5:5)

5. Why must the church purge itself of this sin? (5:6)

Answer these questions by reading 1 Corinthians 6

6. How should disputes among Christians be settled, and how does Paul motivate the Corinthians to handle them in this way? (6:2-6)

7. Why are lawsuits among Christians wrong in principle? (6:7-8)

8. What understanding of the kingdom of God does Paul give in 6:9-11? Who will be included in that kingdom and who will not?

9. How does Paul qualify the statement, "I have the right to do anything," and why does he think it must be qualified? (6:12-14)

10. Why should Christians not engage in prostitution, according to Paul? (6:15-20)

Answer these questions by reading 1 Corinthians 7

11. Why does Paul consider marriage and the marital relationship advisable? (7:2-9)

12. What is Paul's view of celibacy? (7:1, 7-9, 25-35)

13. What is Paul's view of divorce? (7:12-16, 39)

14. Why does Paul want people (circumcised, uncircumcised, slaves, the free, the unmarried, the married) to remain as they were at the time of their conversion to Christ? (7:17-31)

15. What counsel has Paul for persons who are unmarried or widowed? (7:8-9, 39-40)

DIMENSION TWO: WHAT DOES THE BIBLE MEAN?

This section on personal morality in the church deals with several subjects: a case of incest (5:1-8), the relation of Christians within and beyond the church (5:9-13), lawsuits among church members (6:1-11), sexual freedom (6:12-20), and marriage (chapter 7).

■ **1 Corinthians 5:1.** The exact nature of the sin is difficult to determine. In 5:1, the Greek word behind "sexual immorality" means prostitution or traffic with prostitutes; but in the New Testament, the word is often used in the more general sense of irregular sexual conduct of any kind. The kind of irregularity is partly indicated by the latter part of the verse, which in the Greek reads, "a certain one has the woman of his father." In the Greek text, whether she is a wife or a concubine is not clear. Since Paul does not call the sin *adultery* (a different Greek word), it is possible that the father is dead or divorced from the woman. Whether the son (the church member) is married to the woman is also unknown. All we can conclude is that the son has taken a woman with whom his father has had sexual relations. We do not know whether she is a member of the church.

Taking one's father's wife was forbidden among Jews (Leviticus 18:8; 20:11) and condemned by Gentiles, as Paul in indicates, although the practice of it may have been winked at in the loose sexual morality of the Gentile world. Jews who committed this sin were stoned.

■ **1 Corinthians 5:2, 6.** Why the church is "proud" (literally, "puffed up") about the situation must be surmised. The answer is probably that the members, claiming superior knowledge and the supposed freedom that they thought goes with it, are relishing that freedom and proving that, as spiritual persons, they can do what they like with their bodies. In 6:12-20, we learn that consorting with prostitutes was indulged in by some church members.

■ **1 Corinthians 5:3-8.** Paul's words are blunt and his directives sharp. He believes that Christ came to raise the moral level of the world, not to depress it below pagan standards. Not arrogance but mourning is appropriate. The sinful person must be disciplined by removal from the church.

In the synagogues, Jews practiced excommunication for serious ritual or moral offenses. Paul's directions for excommunication are clear. The assembled church is to act. Paul, though absent in body, will be present in spirit. The power of the Lord Jesus will be there. In Jesus' name and by his authority they are to put the man out of the church and hand him over to Satan "for the destruction of the flesh, so that his spirit may be saved on the day of the Lord" (5:5).

To hand him over to Satan apparently means to put him out into the world where Satan exercises his authority, where the forces of destruction are at work, possibly bringing about the man's death.

But Satan, unknowingly, will be doing Christ's work. Just how is not stated. Will the experience bring about repentance and saving faith in Christ? All we know is that Paul expects the discipline to result in the man's salvation at the Day of Judgment. The church's purpose is always redemption, even for serious moral offenders.

Paul's reference to *leaven* (5:6-8) would be readily understood. Leaven or yeast quickly affects the whole lump of dough. Here the leaven is symbolic of sin and evil.

This sin and the boasting over it may have far-reaching effects on the church. Paul now apparently remembers that the Passover and Feast of Unleavened Bread lie just ahead. (He seems to be anticipating the Christian celebration of Passover, which came fifty days before Pentecost, when he would leave Ephesus [16:8].) As the Jews removed every trace of leaven before these festivals (Exodus 12:15) and the eating of the Passover lamb, so the church should remove all evil before it celebrates the death of him who was the true Passover Lamb. The church is dedicated to righteous living ("bread without yeast, the bread of sincerity and truth") and must have nothing to do with "malice and wickedness" (5:8).

■ **1 Corinthians 5:9-13.** Paul now corrects a misunderstanding by the Corinthians of something he had written in his previous letter (now lost; see lesson 6). They thought he had told them to keep away from all immoral people, whereas he meant only immoral people in the church. The church must live in the world, not go out of it; but living in the world, it must yet discipline its members.

■ **1 Corinthians 6:1-11.** Church members are suing one another in pagan courts. Paul again tackles the problem head on. However, his approach is by way of an appeal to conscience. Note the large number of questions he puts to the church, both here and in chapter 5. He wants them to judge for themselves the incongruity of their practice with Christian principle.

Three basic principles underlie Paul's discussion of the problem of lawsuits among Christians:

1. The church should handle its own internal disputes. Jewish communities had their courts for settling internal affairs, as we learn from the Dead Sea Scrolls and other Jewish sources. For God's people, who claim divinely given life standards and the power to live by them, resorting

to pagan judges to settle their squabbles seems to Paul incongruous and humiliating.

2. Bearing a wrong would be better than going to court about it. Paul knew full well Jesus' teaching about non-retaliation to evil (Matthew 5:39-42), as Romans 12:14-21 shows. Since he does not appeal to Jesus' authority directly here, he must have feel that the point does not need proof. It is enough for Paul simply to mention a principle that all Christians know (see 1 Peter 2:19-23).

3. Christians should not be doing wrong at all (6:8-11). The kingdom of God is not a den of thieves, drunkards, sexually immoral persons, adulterers, idolaters, and greedy people, but a fellowship of transformed persons, who in their washing, sanctification, and justification through Jesus Christ and the Holy Spirit have risen to a new kind of life.

■ **1 Corinthians 6:12-20.** The Corinthians apparently had taken as their slogan, "Everything is permissible" for me (see also 10:23). While Paul does not flatly deny that there is truth in the slogan—in fact, they may be quoting something back to him that he had said at Corinth—he hastens to qualify the statement. He does this by three counterbalances: what is helpful, what enslaves, and the proper area of its application.

The "beneficial" is that which builds up, something that Christianity is basically committed to (8:1; Ephesians 4:11-16). Whatever tears down in the exercise of freedom cannot be right.

Neither can the doing of that which enslaves be allowed. To put oneself under any master other than Christ, by practices and habits, is to go back to the old life out of which one has come.

Paul emphatically declares that the slogan certainly does not apply to free sexual gratification. It may properly be applied to food, since the stomach perishes, but not to union with harlots, which union affects the whole person (the meaning of *body* here). The whole person has been united to Christ and is destined to share his resurrection life. To destroy this union by a relationship with harlots in the exercise of freedom is to surrender one's salvation, so dearly bought (6:20), and to dismiss the Holy Spirit from the dwelling place in us.

■ **1 Corinthians 7.** The stage is now set for Paul's discussion of marriage, a subject the Corinthians asked about in a letter to him (7:1).

Two tendencies are at work in the church at Corinth in regard to sex: one is that "anything goes"; and the other is that sex and marriage should be shunned altogether. Paul regards neither view as Christian and in a lengthy section steers between these extremes. His counsel falls into two categories:

1. *Counsel for Unmarried Persons.* Paul regards celibacy as the best state (7:1, 7-8, 26-27), because celibate persons are free to serve the Lord without distraction (7:34-35), and because the end of the age with its accompanying troubles is near (7:28-31).

However, Paul regards marriage as advisable for most people. He sees no evil in it. Certainly one should marry if necessary for the maintenance of virtue (7:2, 9, 36), whether one is at present unmarried (7:1, 8), widowed, or engaged to be married (7:36-38). After the death of a spouse, people are free to remarry if the partner-to-be is a Christian (7:39). Christian people are free to decide for themselves what they will do, as God has no set will for everyone.

2. *Counsel for Married Persons.* The sexual needs of both partners should be met within the marriage relationship (7:3-5). Abstinence by mutual agreement for a period of prayer may be desirable but should not be prolonged (7:5). In view of Christ's explicit command (Mark 10:2-12), there should be no divorce (1 Corinthians 7:10-12). If the wife cannot remain with her husband, she must remain single or be reconciled with her husband (7:11).

Where one partner is Christian and the other not, the union should be kept intact, if possible, in the hope that the unbelieving partner may be won to Christian discipleship

(7:16). Children of a mixed marriage are holy through the holiness of the Christian partner (7:14). In such a marriage, continuance of the relationship must be voluntary (7:15).

Paul regards the end of the age as near (7:29-31) and thinks it best that all, whatever their status, remain as they were at the time of their conversion (7:17-24).

DIMENSION THREE: WHAT DOES THE BIBLE MEAN TO ME?

1 Corinthians 5—Discipline in the Church

Is the church today too indifferent to the moral conduct of its members and too afraid to discipline those who persist in sinful ways? Are we to pass judgment on the conduct of fellow church members? If so, what standard of judgment should we use?

Why should some secular organizations (service clubs, lodges, and so on) maintain standards for their members and the church should not?

Would Jesus have approved of Paul's attitude toward the incestuous man at Corinth?

1 Corinthians 6:1-11— Lawsuits Against Fellow Christians

Should churches today have courts for settling disputes among their members? Newspapers sometimes carry stories about lawsuits brought by churches against their pastors (or vice versa). Do such lawsuits harm the church's life and work? How do they affect you? Are internal courts preferable to external, government associated courts for dealing with issues that arise in the church?

What about Paul and Jesus' principle of non-retaliation? Are there situations in which the application of this principle will work and will not work? Has it worked for you?

1 Corinthians 7—Marriage and Morals

Bertrand Russell said that the Christian church's view, due to Paul's teaching, that "all intercourse outside marriage is immoral" is "based on the view that all sexual intercourse even within marriage is regrettable"—a view that goes, he said, against "biological facts" and is "a moral aberration."[1] Was Russell fair to Paul and the Christian view of sex?

Under what conditions today might celibacy as a lifestyle be advisable?

In view of Paul's teaching about divorce and remarriage, why do most modern churches not follow it? What is/ should be the Christian view of sex in modern times?

---

[1] Bertrand Russell, *Marriage and Morals* (New York: W.W. Norton & Co. 1957), 29.

Knowledge puffs up while love builds up. (8:1)

KNOWLEDGE AND LOVE IN THE CHURCH

1 Corinthians 8:1–11:1

DIMENSION ONE: WHAT DOES THE BIBLE SAY?

Answer these questions by reading 1 Corinthians 8

1. What seem to be the key words or topic addressed in the text of 1 Corinthians 8? What do they indicate about the views of the Corinthians? (8:1-5)

2. Describe persons "with all your knowledge" (8:10) as Paul pictures them: their ideas, their attitudes, and their actions. (All of chapter 8)

3. Describe the "weak brother or sister" (8:11): ideas, attitudes, and actions. (8:7-13)

Answer these questions by reading 1 Corinthians 9

4. What evidence does Paul offer that he is a true apostle? (9:1-2)

5. What rights as an apostle does Paul cite? (9:3-6)

6. List as many reasons as you can find why Paul has not made use of his rights as an apostle. (9:12, 15-27)

7. What "boast" does Paul have? (9:15-18)

8. To what groups of people has Paul become "a slave"? (9:19-22)

9. Why has Paul done this? (9:19-23)

10. What must athletes do to win; and what is the prize Paul is striving for? (9:24-27; Philippians 3:10-14)

Answer these questions by reading 1 Corinthians 10:1–11:1

11. What blessings did the "ancestors" receive in the events connected with the Exodus from Egypt? (10:1-4)

12. Why was God not pleased with most of the ancestors? (10:5-10)

13. What lessons should "we" (Christians) draw from their experience? (10:6-12)

14. What resources do Christians have to keep them from sinning and incurring God's displeasure, as the "ancestors" did? (10:11-13)

15. Why should the Corinthians have nothing to do with the worship of idols and the practice of idolatrous rites? (10:14-22)

16. What is the proper meaning of the cup and the bread for Christians? (10:16-17)

17. What are the Corinthians to do about meat sold in the public markets? (10:25-26)

18. What are they to do when unbelievers invite them to dinner? (10:27-29)

19. What general principles should guide Christians in their relationship with other Christians and with unbelievers? (10:23-11:1)

DIMENSION TWO: WHAT DOES THE BIBLE MEAN?

First Corinthians 8:1–11:1 deals with an ancient problem, but treats it in such a way that the discussion is amazingly relevant to our times and needs.

The question asked by the Corinthians—presumably in their letter to Paul (7:1; 8:1)—concerns the legitimacy for Christians of eating food that has been dedicated to gods in sacred ceremonies at pagan temples, and then consumed at Temple banquets or sold in the marketplace for home consumption. Paul answers this question and, along with it, a much greater one: "Am I my brother's keeper?" (Genesis 4:9). Basically, the section treats the question of individual freedom and social responsibility from the Christian perspective.

■ **1 Corinthians 8:1-3.** Paul begins by quoting something the Corinthians have said to him: "We all possess knowledge." This angers Paul. The Corinthians are idly chattering about their knowledge! They all know that idols represent gods that do not exist, and that they have the right to eat meat that was dedicated to these gods.

The swagger behind the statement (see 8:2) leads Paul to bring them down a few notches right at the beginning of his discussion. "Knowledge puffs up while love builds up," he says. Knowing about God and the gods (8:4) is not the important thing. Loving God and being known (recognized and accepted) by God is. Loveless knowledge is good for nothing, according to Paul. (See 13:2.)

■ **1 Corinthians 8:4-6.** Paul agrees that "there is no God but one." This knowledge is important. To this extent the Corinthians have learned well. They have turned away from the "so-called gods" to the "one God, the Father," who is creator of all things, and to the "one Lord, Jesus Christ," God's instrument in creation and redemption, and have become a chosen and redeemed people.

■ **1 Corinthians 8:7-13.** But the Corinthians' claim that "we all possess knowledge" is too sweeping. Actually, some Corinthians do not. They regard the food as somehow contaminated by association with pagan rites in pagan temples, as if false gods really exist.

Paul calls them "the weak" (8:9). They cannot rid themselves of the feeling that they are worshiping a false god when they eat food that has been dedicated to a pagan god. And when they see "you, with all your knowledge" eating this food in a pagan temple (perhaps at a banquet of a trade guild), they are emboldened to eat it too (at home or in their own trade-guild banquets). Doing what they believe to be wrong violates their conscience and destroys them (puts them under guilt). The bold act of "you, with all your knowledge" thus results in a sin against other Christians and a sin against God.

The point is that knowledge may give us rights, but love may require that we give up those rights. We are our brother's and sister's keeper and are not free to do what we like without regard to its effect on others. Food would be a little thing to give up to keep a brother or sister from falling.

■ **1 Corinthian 9:1-14.** In 1 Corinthians 8, Paul has laid down the principle that knowledge, which leads to rights and freedoms, must be controlled by love for others. Otherwise, it will puff up the knower, wreck the more unenlightened, and eventually destroy the church.

In chapter 9, Paul uses himself as an example of the control of knowledge and rights by love. He knows that he is completely free, as a Christian and a Roman citizen, and has no reason to knuckle under to anyone, especially to "weak" Christians. Furthermore, he is an apostle of Jesus Christ, made so in a face-to-face meeting with Jesus on the Damascus road (Galatians 1:15-16). The Corinthians are the fruits and validation of his apostleship. If anyone has "knowledge" and "rights," Paul has them!

Paul now mentions some of his rights: to food and drink (or perhaps to eat and drink what he pleases), to be married and accompanied by a wife, and to refrain from working for a living.

Proof that he has these rights consists of the practice of other apostles (9:5-6); comparison with other fields of labor (soldiers, vinedressers, shepherds, and priests [9:7, 13]); the law of Moses (9:8-10); and the express command of the Lord Jesus (9:14).

But Paul has not made use of these rights because the spread and effectiveness of the gospel would be hindered by exercising them (9:12), and he would be denied the satisfaction of preaching the gospel free of charge (9:16-18). Such surrender of rights serves positively to both advance the gospel with many different groups (slaves, Jews, those under the law, those outside the law, the weak, all persons [9:19-22]), and to ensure that Paul may be saved at the last by reaching the goal himself (9:23-27).

■ **1 Corinthians 10:1-22.** This section seeks to drive home Paul's argument that knowledge and the rights that flow from knowledge must be carefully controlled, if spiritual disaster is not to ensue.

First, he appeals to the Old Testament (10:1-13). By engaging in uncontrolled freedom, the people of Israel, after their marvelous deliverance from Egypt and their high spiritual experiences, fell into gross immorality and did not inherit the Promised Land (10:1-5). The Corinthians should beware lest their lust for sex, food, and other freedoms— based on their rights—put them under God's end-time judgment (10:6-11). Disaster need not come to them, as God will help them resist temptation, if they humble themselves (10:12-13).

Second, Paul appeals to the Corinthians' common sense (10:14-22). By participating in the cup and bread of Holy Communion, they have entered into an exclusive union with Christ and with one another, like the union the people of Israel formed with God by eating the sacrifices at the altar. This unity can be destroyed by dabbling in pagan rites and practices, behind which there are demonic powers. Which table do they want to be a part of: Christ's or the demons'? They can't be a part of both.

■ **1 Corinthians 10:23–11:1.** These verses offer conclusions to the whole section (8:1–11:1). Briefly, they are as follows: concentrate on what is helpful to all, not simply on what is lawful for oneself (10:23-24). All food belongs to God and is given by God for our eating, therefore, the Corinthians may eat whatever meat is sold in the marketplace, regardless of its origin (10:25- 26). In the home of an unbeliever a Christian should not inquire about the origin of the food, but eat what is served, so that no one is hurt by this eating (10:27-29). In sum, do everything to honor God, to advance the salvation of all people, and to imitate Paul and Jesus Christ (10:31–11:1).

DIMENSION THREE: WHAT DOES THE BIBLE MEAN TO ME?

1 Corinthians 8:7-13—Rights and Love

What do you think you have a right to do, whether other Christians like it or not? Have you been doing certain questionable things without really considering their effect on others? Has your "knowledge" puffed you up, or has your love built others up?

1 Corinthians 9:15-22—Rights Surrendered

What rights have you sacrificed for the sake of winning others to Christ and building them up in him? Has this sacrifice turned you sour, or do you glory in your privilege of doing something far beyond what is expected of you?

1 Corinthians 10:14-22—Rights and Demons

Have you been trying to go two ways at once: eating at Christ's table and also at the table of demons? What sinful things that are inconsistent with your Christian beliefs and witness are you tolerating in your life?

Now you are the body of Christ, and each one of you is a part of it. (12:27)

WORSHIP IN THE CHURCH (PART 1)

1 Corinthians 11:2–12:31

DIMENSION ONE: WHAT DOES THE BIBLE SAY?

Answer these questions by reading 1 Corinthians 11:2-16

1. Is Paul in sympathy with the Corinthian practice of allowing women to participate actively in church worship services? (11:3-16)

2. What is the order of authority (we might say chain of command) in the universe, as Paul sees it? (11:3)

Answer these questions by reading 1 Corinthians 11:17-34

3. What criticisms does Paul make of the way the Corinthians conduct themselves at "the Lord's Supper"? (11:18-22)

4. What similarities and what differences are there between Paul's account of the Last Supper and Mark's account? (11:23-26; Mark 14:22-25)

5. How should the Corinthians prepare themselves for eating the Lord's Supper? (11:28, 34)

6. What consequences have followed and will follow the unworthy eating of the Lord's Supper? (11:27, 29-30)

Answer these questions by reading 1 Corinthians 12:1-11

7. What test does Paul suggest for determining whether a person has the Holy Spirit or some other spirit? (12:2-3)

8. Where do spiritual gifts come from? (12:4-6, 11)

9. What is the purpose of these gifts? (12:7)

10. What kinds of gifts are there? (12:8-10)

Answer these questions by reading 1 Corinthians 12:12-31

11. What characteristics does the body of Christ possess, and how did it get that way? (12:12-13)

12. What parts of the human body does Paul refer to in his analogy? (12:15-24)

13. Why does Paul refer to all these parts of the body? (12:14-16)

14. What are the differences between the two lists of kinds of gifts? (12:8-10, 28-30)

15. Is one person supposed to have all these gifts, and is any one gift to be possessed by all? (12:29-30)

DIMENSION TWO: WHAT DOES THE BIBLE MEAN?

■ **1 Corinthians 11:2-16.** The Corinthians dramatically carried out their belief that they "have the right to do anything" by applauding the incestuous man, by the general "hell raising" that led to lawsuits, by patronizing prostitutes, by the bravado shown in their eating in the temples of idols, and by their general lack of concern for others and for self-discipline. This spirit of "freedom" also manifested in various ways in the worship life of the church.

One way was a push by the women of the church for equality with men. The women were removing the symbol of their subordination and the mark of their modesty—their veils—and participating with bare heads in the exhorting and praying in the services of worship.

Paul evidently had taught at Corinth what he told the Galatians: "There is neither Jew nor Gentile . . . nor male and female, for you are all one in Christ Jesus" (Galatians 3:28). Furthermore, their belief that they were experiencing now the life of the kingdom of God (1 Corinthians 4:8), in which gender distinctions would no longer exist, emboldened the women to act out the freedom they had been promised as Christians.

Since Christian worship at this stage was held in private homes (Romans 16:5; Philemon 1), it is possible that the women felt they should have the freedom from the veil they normally enjoyed at home. And their seeming lack of modesty in exposing their heads to men other than their husbands may have stemmed from the new "family" character of Christianity.

But Paul sees in the laying aside of the veil a threat to God-established order and possibly to the morals and reputation of the church. Women of good character covered their heads in public; prostitutes did not. Apparently some church members at Corinth did not approve of what the women were doing, or they would not have told Paul about it.

Paul's position seems to be that equality before God is quite consistent with social subordination.

In advising that all Christians should stay in the status they were in at the time of their conversion, Paul says that one may be a slave and still be free in Christ, and that the free person is actually a slave of Christ (1 Corinthians 7:20-24). Paul launches no attack on the institution of slavery, though he sows the seed of a new order yet to spring up (Treat a slave as a "dear brother" [Philemon 16; see Galatians 3:28].) Paul believes that, in the short time before the end time, a change of status is not advisable (1 Corinthians 7:17-24); and this conclusion he now applies to women.

Paul would be quite willing to grant that when the kingdom of God actually comes in glory, and not simply in anticipation, all distinctions of rank and sex will vanish. But the great day has not yet come (2 Thessalonians 2:1-5). Meanwhile, we must maintain appropriate social structures and conventions (Romans 13:1-17).

■ **1 Corinthians 11:17-26.** Paul's mild attempt at complimenting the Corinthians (11:2) is short-lived. He soon turns to bitter and ironic censure.

The common meals of the church have become a dis-grace. At these meals, people have formed cliques, perhaps both doctrinal and social. Possibly the followers of the respective leaders (1:11-12) gravitate together, though Paul seems to indicate here that the division is between rich and poor. Whatever the exact cause, Paul is horrified that factions should appear at the Lord's Supper. Here are taken the bread and the wine by which the church is constituted and recognized as "one body" (10:17).

Even more horrifying is the callous disregard of the poor at these meals. Some of the eaters are gluttonous and become drunk; others have little or nothing to eat or drink. The wealthier apparently have brought an abundance of food, which they forthwith gobble up without sharing with the less fortunate. Verse 33 seems to imply that the working poor find it difficult to arrive on time; and when they appear, little or no food is left.

These meals are a continuation of the common meals in the earliest church (Acts 2:42, 46), which in turn continued Jesus' meals with his disciples (Mark 2:15-17; 6:35-44; 14:17-25). Joyful communion was part of these meals, since Jesus and his followers seem to have viewed them as anticipations of the great banquet soon to be held in the kingdom of God (Matthew 8:11).

The last meal before Jesus' death took on a somewhat different character, partly because it was connected with the Passover celebration, and partly because of the personal tragedy that lay ahead of Jesus.

While among the Jews this dinner (Passover) joyfully commemorates the events of the Exodus and looks forward to the greater deliverance the Messiah will bring, for Jesus and his disciples it was a more somber meal, whose elements Jesus interpreted in special ways. The broken bread became his body and the wine his blood, both given to seal a new covenant between God and God's people. Jesus seems to have regarded himself as the Passover lamb, whose death would be redemptive. He looked forward to meeting the disciples again at a banquet in the coming kingdom of God (Mark 14:25); and he may have wanted the disciples to meet together continuously in table fellowship in memory of his sacrificial act and in anticipation of his coming again.

At Corinth, and perhaps at other places in the Gentile world, the deep meaning of the meal has faded, if indeed it ever really was understood. The Lord's Supper has become an occasion for gluttony by some, and it no longer reflects and promotes the deep unity of the Christian fellowship. Paul seeks here to put meaning back into the supper.

For Paul, the meal is commemorative in nature. It looks back to Jesus' sacrificial self-giving, as the Passover lamb (1 Corinthians 5:7), to establish the new covenant and to proclaim the meaning of his death until he comes again. The meal should be observed in appreciation of all this.

■ **1 Corinthians 11:27-34.** These verses contain a warning against eating the Lord's Supper unworthily, in a greedy and partisan way. To do so is to sin against the Lord's sacrificial offering of himself on our behalf, to put ourselves outside the effects of this death, and to incur God's judgment, now and in the future.

Paul may view the present judgment mentioned here—sickness and death (11:30)—as the consequence of self-exclusion from the benefits of salvation, brought on by the ensuing attacks of the powers of evil, as in the case of the incestuous man (5:5).

Therefore, before we eat, we should examine our attitudes and conduct and satisfy our urgent physical needs at home, before arriving for the Lord's Supper.

■ **1 Corinthians 12:1-3.** Paul now turns to another subject about which the Corinthians inquired in their letter: spiritual gifts. The Corinthians made much of their gifts and disputed among themselves about their relative importance.

In chapter 12, Paul treats three aspects of the subject: the proper test of the source of gifts (12:1-3); the character and purpose of the gifts (12:4-11); and the relation of members with different gifts to one another in the body of Christ (the church, 12:12-31).

A test of the source of spiritual manifestations is needed at Corinth because many have claimed to be possessed by the spirit of some god, swept away into frenzied speech in worship. Some of them may have cried in or out of the Christian assembly, 'Jesus be cursed!" while claiming divine inspiration. How is one to know who really has the Spirit of God?

Paul's answer is that the content of what is said identifies its origin as from the Holy Spirit or from some demonic spirit. Since it is the Holy Spirit's work to glorify Jesus (see John 15:26; 16:14), and since the confession of the lordship of Jesus, along with belief in the heart, is the doorway into salvation (Romans 10:9), anyone who exalts Jesus in this way must have the Holy Spirit. Anyone who debases Jesus must have some other spirit.

■ **1 Corinthians 12:4-11.** All spiritual gifts come from the same source, variously identified as "the same Spirit," "the same Lord," and "the same God." Here we have the raw material for a doctrine of the Trinity (God, Jesus Christ, the Holy Spirit).

The gifts are diverse. Some are associated with the mind (wisdom, knowledge), some with the will (special faith, healing, miracles), and some with speech (prophecy, the ability to distinguish speakers with the Holy Spirit from those with another spirit, speaking in tongues, and the interpretation of tongues). Another list of the types of gifts appears in 12:28-30.

■ **1 Corinthians 12:12-30.** In explaining the relationship of members with different gifts to one another and to the whole church, Paul draws on an analogy long used in the Greek world: the human body as the symbol of unity. By the Holy Spirit's work in baptism, many diverse people have been drawn into the unity of Christ's body, and all have been empowered by that Spirit.

Though a new unity has been created, there is yet diversity, as there is in the human body. All bodily members are essential, whether they are more honored or less honored parts, all have their unique functions, all work together for the good of the whole body. So all the members of the church—with their differing gifts and functions—are to work together for the common good. Discord is to give way to mutual care and mutual rejoicing (12:25-26).

DIMENSION THREE: WHAT DOES THE BIBLE MEAN TO ME?

1 Corinthians 11:2-16—Men and Women in the Church

Paul was certainly far ahead of the Jews of his time in his attitude toward women. His statement in Galatians 3:28 is revolutionary in nature; and his praise and recognition of women in Romans 16:1-4, 6, 12, 13, 15, along with his frequent close association with them (Acts 16:13-15; 18:1-3), remind us of the attitude of Jesus toward women. In 1 Corinthians 11:2-16, Paul asserts the right of women to prophesy, preach, and pray in the church meetings. Paul is against the easy divorce of women by men (7:10-11), widely allowed in Judaism. He has a high view of the place of women in the home, comparing husband-wife union to that between Christ and the church (Ephesians 5:31-33). The popular view of our time that Paul was "a woman-hater" cannot withstand investigation.

With what emphases in the women's movements of our time do you think Paul would be in sympathy if he were living today? What might he oppose? What should the Christian response be to the shifting understanding of women's roles in the church and in society?

1 Corinthians 11:17-34—The Lord's Supper

The bread and the cup were taken originally in connection with an actual meal of gathered Christians. What would be gained for the church if the communion elements were restored to their original context, and what might be lost?

What has the Communion service meant to you in your Christian life? What might Paul's interpretation of the Lord's Supper do to your understanding and experience of it? Some people find the whole thing boring and do not attend church when Holy Communion is being observed. What might be done to make it more meaningful and helpful?

1 Corinthians 12:1-31—Spiritual Gifts

What does the Holy Spirit mean to you? How do you conceive of the Spirit's relationship to God and Jesus Christ? Have you experienced the Holy Spirit in any way?

How are the Holy Spirit's gifts related to the natural talents with which we all were born? Are these released, heightened, and made effective by the Spirit, or are the Spirit's gifts of an entirely different character?

Now I know in part; then I shall know fully, even as I am fully known. (1 Corinthians 13:12)

WORSHIP IN THE CHURCH (PART 2) / THE RESURRECTION

1 Corinthians 13–15

DIMENSION ONE: WHAT DOES THE BIBLE SAY?

Answer these questions by reading 1 Corinthians 13

1. With what subject does chapter 12 end; and with what subject does chapter 14 begin? After reading chapter 13, what can you say about the way it fits into its context? (1 Corinthians 12:27-31; 13; 14:1-5)

2. What is the main idea of each paragraph in 1 Corinthians 13? (13:1-3, 4-7, 8-12, 13)

3. If you had only 1 Corinthians 13 by which to define *love*, how would you define it?

Answer these questions by reading 1 Corinthians 14

4. What does Paul mean by the gift of prophecy in 1 Corinthians 14? (14:3-4, 6, 22, 24, 31)

5. What does Paul mean by the gift of tongues in 1 Corinthians 14? (14:2, 4, 14, 21-23, 28)

6. How do prophecy and tongues compare in value for oneself and for the church as a whole? (14:1-6, 12, 14, 18-24, 27-28, 31, 39)

7. What suggestions does Paul give for improving the worship services at Corinth? (14:14-16, 26-40)

Answer these questions by reading 1 Corinthians 15

8. Why does Paul discuss the subject of resurrection in this letter? (15:12)

9. How seriously does Paul take the attitude of those mentioned in 15:12? (15:1-2, 13-19, 29-34)

10. How does Paul establish the reality of the resurrection of Jesus? (15:3-10)

11. What is the place and function of the Resurrection in the plan of God? (15:20-28)

12. What is the nature of the resurrection body, and why does Paul refer to the different kinds of flesh and bodies in the universe? (15:35-44)

13. What contrasts does Paul draw between the two Adams? (15:45-49)

14. What result will follow the future coming of Christ? (15:50-57)

15. What consequence for daily living does faith in the Resurrection and the coming of Christ have? (15:58)

DIMENSION TWO: WHAT DOES THE BIBLE MEAN?

One of the great passages in all literature is 1 Corinthians 13. It sparkles like a gem in the midst of a rather prosaic passage about an ancient problem at Corinth: a squabble about the relative value of the gifts or abilities church members there possessed.

For Paul, *love* is God's graciousness manifested in the gift of Jesus Christ to benefit and save undeserving humans (Romans 5:6-8). God bestows this love on persons who respond to the love he expressed in Jesus Christ (Romans 5:5). In imitation of God's love, Christians are to show graciousness toward the undeserving.

Love, then, is graciousness, kindness, generosity, and mercy toward the undeserving, even toward enemies (Romans 12:9- 10, 14-21).

■ **1 Corinthians 13:1-3.** Paul speaks first about the necessity of love. Without love, even the most dramatic and coveted gifts are valueless: human and angelic tongues, prophecy (the declaration of the divine will in preaching), omniscience (all knowledge), and mountain-moving faith. Even acts like the giving away all of one's goods and offering oneself as a burnt sacrifice in martyrdom may stem from motives other than love. Unless love prompts and directs the use of these dramatic gifts and activities, they are worth nothing.

■ **1 Corinthians 13:4-7.** Paul writes next about the characteristics of love: first, what it is; second, what it is not; and third, again what it is.

The person who loves is patient (long-suffering), kind (gentle in behavior), not envious (jealous), not boastful, not proud (puffed up), not rude (ill-mannered), not self-seeking, not easily angered, not resentful (does not keep track of wrongs), not delighting in evil (unrighteousness).

The description concludes with strong positives: love rejoices over right (truth); bears (supports) all things; believes all things (keeps faith strong); hopes all things (is strongly optimistic); endures all things (perseveres in hardship).

■ **1 Corinthians 13:8-13.** Paul concludes by celebrating the permanence of love. Love alone endures. Prophecy, tongues, knowledge, and belonging to this finite world are limited and transient. At the coming of the infinite (perfect) order, they will be left behind, like childhood knowledge and speech give way to the maturity of adulthood.

Some things will last forever: faith (trust in God), hope (openness to the future), and love (God's love for us and our love for God and one another). These will be more alive in the perfect order than they are here. And above them all towers *love* (that which God essentially is—1 John 4:8).

■ **1 Corinthians 14:1-25.** Paul gives a lengthy comparison of two gifts (prophecy and tongues) in 14:1-25. The Corinthians are putting too much emphasis on speaking in tongues to the detriment of what Paul calls "the greater gifts" (12:31). Paul believes that both prophecy and teaching are of greater value than tongues for the upbuilding of the church, as his order of gifts in chapter 12 and the contents of chapter 14 show.

Paul exalts prophecy throughout chapter 14. It is soon clear from his discussion that he is not thinking of prophecy as prediction of future events but as the speaking of God's message to the church.

Paul describes tongues as a speaking to God and to oneself (14:2, 28), which builds up the speaker and not the church (14:4). Tongues is the language of prayer, which proceeds from the spirit but not from the mind (14:14). Paul writes that he prefers to pray with both the spirit and the mind (14:15).

Without interpretation, speaking in tongues is not understandable, even by fellow Christians, and may lead non-church members to think that those who speak in tongues are "out of [their] mind" (14:23). It deals with "mysteries" (14:2), God and the person speaking in tongues sharing hidden truths. Tongues is a judging sign for unbelievers, who are chastised by having to hear words they cannot understand (14:21-22).

But Paul does not entirely denigrate tongues. He includes it at the end of his listing of the gifts. He says that he speaks in tongues "more than all of you" (14:18), and he wants all to speak in tongues (14:5). Private speaking to God and building oneself up have value. But the church service is not the place to do this (14:19), unless the tongues are interpreted for the benefit of others (14:5, 13, 27).

If, by interpretation, tongues can be turned into prophecy (declaring God's message), then it will have value for the assembled congregation. But if no one is present to interpret, tongues-speakers should keep silent and carry on their conversation with God in private (14:28).

■ **1 Corinthians 14:26-40.** Paul gives suggestions for improving the character of the worship services at Corinth in these verses.

Paul mentions several elements of the service: a hymn, a word of instruction, a revelation, a tongue, an interpretation (14:26). Tongues-speaking should be done by two or three in turn, if an interpreter is present; otherwise, there should be no tongues-speaking. Two or three prophets (declarers of God's message) should speak, all hearers weighing what is said. Any church member may speak God's word to the congregation in proper order (14:31).

Women are not to disturb the service with chatter or irrelevant questions. They are to reserve the latter for answer at home (14:34-36). (Paul cannot have meant here to deny their right to prophesy and pray publicly, a right asserted by him in 11:2-16.)

In sum, the mind, not the emotions, should guide the services. We should strive for orderliness, not confusion. An atmosphere of learning must be maintained. Spontaneity in speaking, singing, and sounding the "Amen" (14:16) should characterize the worship. Free and orderly participation should be encouraged. The purpose of all is to "build up the church" (14:12).

■ **1 Corinthians 15:1-11.** Some of the Corinthians were skeptical of, if not downright hostile to, the idea of the resurrection of dead people (15:12). There probably were several reasons:

1. Many knowledgeable people of the first century regarded claims and stories about life beyond the grave as little better than old tales and legends. They held death to be the natural end of life.

2. Others, like Plato and Seneca, believed in the survival of the soul but not the body. The body belonged to the perishing material order, but the soul to a higher eternal order.

3. The Corinthian Christians believed that they had entered into eternal life through their baptism and participation in the Lord's Supper, and were enjoying the fruits of their new life now (4:8). Nothing more was to be expected.

Even in Judaism, there was controversy about life after death. The Pharisees believed in it, including the resurrection of the body; but the Sadducees did not (Acts 23:6-8), because it was not clearly taught in the Law of Moses (the Pentateuch).

Paul had a formidable task on his hands to convince the Corinthians of not only the reality of life beyond the grave but also the resurrection of the body as well as of the spirit. The clincher for Paul was the resurrection of Jesus, which he sets out here to prove. His argument is fourfold:

1. Jesus' resurrection is the fulfillment of the Scripture.

2. He really died and was buried.

3. Subsequent to Jesus' death and burial, he appeared to a large array of people, some of them important, like Cephas (Peter) and James.

4. He appeared to Paul and commissioned Paul to be an apostle.

■ **1 Corinthians 15:12-34.** After arguing for the resurrection of Jesus, Paul tries to establish the certainty of the resurrection of believers. His main arguments are as follows:

1. The resurrection of Jesus and the resurrection of believers are logically consistent. If one happened, the other will.

2. To deny the reality of resurrection is to deny the truth of the gospel.

3. The purpose and consequence of Christ's resurrection are marvelous to contemplate: Christ is the first fruit of those who will be resurrected at his coming; as Adam's sin brought death, Christ's resurrection will bring life; Christ's resurrection leads to his final conquest of the powers of evil (including death).

4. If there is no resurrection from death, some things are sheer foolishness: to be baptized on behalf of dead people; to suffer bitterly, as Paul does, for the Christian enterprise.

5. You must not keep company with people who live for this life only and do not believe in the Resurrection.

■ **1 Corinthians 15:35-58.** The final section of the chapter deals with the nature of the resurrection body. If believers are going to be raised, what sort of existence will they have? Paul answers as follows:

1. Since God has an appropriate body (form of being) for all created beings and objects in their particular habitats, God will give us the sort of body appropriate to our new and glorious stage of existence.

2. Our future existence will not be physical (earthly) but spiritual (heavenly) in character, not fashioned after the likeness of the "earthly man" (Adam), but after "the heavenly man" (Jesus Christ).

3. At the coming of Christ, both the living and the dead will be transformed, since neither the living nor the dead can go into the kingdom of God as they are.

4. The transformation of both the living and the dead will constitute Christ's final victory over death, sin, and the law (which offers sin its opportunity [Romans 7:5, 8]).

The chapter ends with an appeal for steadfastness in faith and labor. The hope of resurrection has firm foundation, and toil in and for the Lord will not be empty of meaning.

DIMENSION THREE: WHAT DOES THE BIBLE MEAN TO ME?

1 Corinthians 13—Christian Love

What meanings can you list for the word *love* as we use it today in our conversation, literature, entertainment, and so on? Compare these meanings with Paul's in 1 Corinthians 13. Might there be better English words than love for what Paul means? If so, suggest a few.

1 Corinthians 14—Christian Worship

Compare and contrast early Christian worship, as Paul describes it in chapter 14, with worship in your church. What elements from that worship might strengthen yours, and what elements might be inadvisable?

What is the proper balance between reason and emotion in worship according to Paul? What place do you think both should have in worship today?

1 Corinthians 15—The Christian Hope

Paul firmly joins the truth of the resurrection of Jesus and the truth of the Christian faith (15:17). Is this an exaggeration? Are the ethical teachings of Jesus and Paul untrue if Jesus was not raised from the dead? What is the relation of ethics to the problem of human sin, and what is the relation of Jesus' resurrection to that problem?

But thanks be to God, who always leads us as captives in Christ's triumphal procession. (2:14)

INTEGRITY UNDER THE NEW COVENANT

2 Corinthians 1–3

DIMENSION ONE: WHAT DOES THE BIBLE SAY?

Answer these questions by reading 2 Corinthians 1:1–2:13

1. What do the following passages tell us about Timothy: Acts 16:1-3; 18:1-5; 1 Corinthians 4:17; 16:10-11; Philippians 2:19-22?

2. To what readers is Second Corinthians addressed? (1:1b)

3. For what does Paul give thanks? (1:3-11)

4. What is Paul's view of suffering? (1:3-7)

5. What does Paul say about the nature of his suffering in Asia (that is, in the Roman province of Asia)? (1:8-10)

6. Against what criticism does Paul defend himself? (1:12-17)

7. How does Paul's characterization of God, of Christ, and of himself refute this criticism? (1:18-22)

8. Why has Paul not come to Corinth as he had planned? (1:23-2:2)

9. What does Paul say about a letter he wrote to the Corinthians? (2:3-4, 9; 7:8, 12)

10. What is Paul's attitude, and what should be the attitude of the Corinthians, toward the person who caused Paul pain at Corinth? (2:5-11)

Answer these questions by reading 2 Corinthians 2:14–3:18

11. What opposite effects does the preaching of the gospel have upon hearers? (2:14-16)

12. What basic contrasts and results are there between the old and new covenants? (3:3-6)

13. Why does the new covenant have more glory than the old? (3:7-11)

14. Why did Moses wear a veil over his face? (3:13)

15. What is it that the Israelites of Paul's day fail to understand? (3:14-16)

16. What results from turning to the Lord? (3:16-18)

DIMENSION TWO: WHAT DOES THE BIBLE MEAN?

Paul's letters to the Corinthians were four or five in number, judging by indications in the letters we have. Here is a listing of these letters:

Letter A—Concerning non-association with immoral Christians (mentioned in 1 Corinthians 5:9, but not preserved);

Letter B—Our First Corinthians;

Letter C—A painful letter (mentioned in 2 Corinthians 2:3-4, 9; 7:8, 12; also not preserved);

Letter D—Our 2 Corinthians (as a whole or only chapters 1–9);

Letter E—Our 2 Corinthians 10–13 (if not part of Letter D).

For several reasons, we suspect that our Second Corinthians consists of two letters, which were joined by the person who gathered Paul's letters together around the end of the first century. The strongest of these reasons is the almost inexplicable change of tone between chapters 1–9 (in which Paul is thankful for his reconciliation with the Corinthians and asks for their help with an offering for the Jerusalem Christians), and chapters 10–13 (where his scolding of them assumes that no reconciliation has been achieved, or that the reconciliation has soured due to new factors in the Corinthian situation). If two letters were joined together to form our present Second Corinthians, the ending of the first and the opening of the second were dropped.

■ **2 Corinthians 1:1-2.** Timothy and Silvanus (Silas) helped Paul found the church at Corinth (Acts 18:5; 2 Corinthians 1:19), and Paul sent Timothy and Titus there at different times to help the church with its problems.

The letter is addressed to all the churches of the Roman province of Achaia, as well as to Corinth. This is because the issue with which it chiefly deals (whether Paul is a true or false apostle) is apparently of concern to all the churches of the region, since they all stem from Paul's mission there.

■ **2 Corinthians 1:3-11.** Paul usually gives thanks at the beginning of his letters for something he knows about his readers. The thanksgiving may include mention of their faith in the Lord Jesus Christ, the spiritual gifts they have received, and the love they have shown toward others. Striking exceptions are the Letter to the Galatians, which begins with an astonished rebuke of the Galatians for their acceptance of a false gospel, and this Letter to the Corinthians.

Here Paul begins by using the Jewish blessing form, in which God, rather than the readers, is praised. Apparently, Paul uses this form because he has little good to say about the Corinthians at this point in their relationship, and because he has recently been rescued by God from a life-threatening experience at Ephesus (2:8-1 0). Praise of God for the deliverance is fresh in his mind and makes an appropriate beginning for a letter to people he can hardly commend.

This blessing contains a striking theological concept. Christian suffering is God's way of comforting the sufferers so that they can share the comfort they have received with others who are suffering. Paul is overflowing with comfort and wants to share his comfort with the Corinthians, if they suffer in the same cause for which he suffers.

But the fellowship of suffering includes more than Paul and the Corinthians. Together they are sharing in Christ's sufferings and in the comfort he provides through the power of his resurrection (Philippians 3:10). God's comfort thus flows to Paul and the Corinthians through Christ's victory over his sufferings. This is in line with Paul's view of Christ: all of God's blessings flow to believers through Christ (1:20).

■ **2 Corinthians 1:12–2:2.** Paul takes up first the Corinthians' general attitude of suspicion and mistrust of him. Some, at least, have regarded him as insincere—particularly in his letters (1:13; 10:9-11)—as acting with the kind of deceitfulness one finds in worldly minded people. Paul hastens to inform them that his conscience assures him that he has behaved toward them and all persons with Godlike sincerity, and he suggests that "the day of the Lord Jesus" (Judgment Day) will confirm this.

After these general remarks, Paul discusses a specific charge of duplicity: his failure to carry out his promise of a visit to Corinth on his way to Macedonia. Instead, he had gone the shorter route, through Troas and straight across the sea to Macedonia. To the Corinthians it looked as if he really did not care about them but did whatever served his convenience and selfish interests.

Paul's answer to the charge of double talk and irresponsible conduct centers on his picture of God, of Christ, and of Paul's mission as a representative of God and Christ. God is faithful; God can be relied on. Jesus Christ, God's Son, is likewise trustworthy. As there is no double talking and double-dealing in God and Christ, so there is no double talking and double-dealing in their commissioned representatives ("me and Silas and Timothy"). God, furthermore, acknowledged these representatives as trustworthy servants by giving them the Holy Spirit as "a deposit" (that is, as the down payment on their coming inheritance in the kingdom of God).

What then was Paul's motive in changing his plans? He wanted to spare the Corinthians another painful visit. Since the writing of our First Corinthians, he apparently had gone from Ephesus to Corinth to settle the problems in his relationship with the church there, only to be rebuffed, rejected, and perhaps slandered by some unknown person, to the pain of himself and the church (2:5-11; 7:12). Paul did not want to repeat a visit of this kind. So he changed his plans, not out of underhanded, selfish interests, but out of concern for the Corinthians and for himself.

■ **2 Corinthians 2:3-13.** Paul now mentions a letter he had written the Corinthians out of anguish of heart and with tears (2:3-4, 9; 7:8, 12). It seems that this letter was written from Ephesus after he returned from his fruitless visit to Corinth.

This must have been a stinging letter, containing demands for disciplining the person who had insulted Paul when he was there (2:5-11; 7:12). Paul regretted for a time that he had sent it (7:8), but it turned out to be effective (7:9-11). At some point after the dispatch of this letter (unless Titus himself carried it), Titus was sent to Corinth to check up on the situation. As chapter 7 tells us, Titus reported to Paul in Macedonia that Paul's demands had been met and that the Christians were reconciled to him.

In 2:5-10, Paul asks for the forgiveness of the offender, who has been punished enough "by the majority." This term may imply that a discordant minority was still against disciplining the offending person. What the discipline was we do not know. Forgiveness is the only possible attitude one can take "in the sight of Christ" (2:10). Not to forgive is to give Satan his chance!

■ **2 Corinthians 2:14–3:6.** Paul's thanksgiving for the triumphant spread of the gospel is perhaps caused by Titus's good report concerning the repentance of the Corinthians and their reconciliation with Paul (7:5-13).

The apostles who preach the gospel have an awesome responsibility: forcing a decision for Christ or against Christ. But knowing that they have been commissioned by God and are doing their work under God's watchful eye, they press on with their fateful work.

False apostles (those who "peddle the word of God for profit") may need letters of recommendation. Not so true

53

apostles. The only letters of recommendation they need are their converts, on whose hearts the Holy Spirit has written a message for all people to read.

True apostles are not self-appointed and self-equipped. Their adequacy for their mission derives from their appointment and equipment by God. Their ministry is exercised under a new, spiritual, life-giving covenant, not under a death-dealing written code.

■ **2 Corinthians 3:7-18.** Paul means for the contrast between the new covenant and the old covenant to validate his and his associates' ministry as opposed to that of other preachers who have come to Corinth. These others obviously have viewed the written code differently from Paul and therefore have preached and ministered differently. Paul now shows that the basis of his ministry is superior to theirs.

The old covenant was "on tablets of stone" and therefore external in nature; the new is "on tablets of human hearts" (3:3) and therefore internal. The old brought condemnation and death; the new brings righteousness and life (3:6-9). The old has transient splendor; the new has greater and permanent splendor (3:7-11). The ministers of the old covenant, from Moses "to this day," have a spirit of timidity and concealment, for they serve a transient, fading, and ineffective covenant; while the ministers of the new covenant are courageous, open, free, and confident in the knowledge that the new covenant brings life and Godlikeness (3:12-18).

DIMENSION THREE: WHAT DOES THE BIBLE MEAN?

2 Corinthians 1:3-11—Christian Suffering

How can we share in Christ's sufferings? Can you give instances when you feel that you have done this? How can we know that our sufferings are really for Christ and not because of our own failures and wrongdoings? What spiritual benefits have you received through your suffering?

2 Corinthians 2:5-11—Forgiveness

Paul wanted the Corinthian offender both punished and forgiven. Was he inconsistent in this? In a Christian context, what is the function of punishment? How are wrath and love related in the character of God, according to the Bible? What was Jesus' attitude toward and practice of forgiveness? Why are "Christians" often so unforgiving?

We do not lose heart. (4:1)

7

MINISTRY UNDER THE NEW COVENANT

2 Corinthians 4:1–6:13

DIMENSION ONE: WHAT DOES THE BIBLE SAY?

Answer these questions by reading 2 Corinthians 4:1–5:10

1. What charges is Paul defending himself against in 4:1-6?

2. How does Paul explain the unbelief of those who reject the gospel? (4:3-4)

3. What is the content of the apostles' gospel, and what is their way of presenting it? (4:1-6)

4. Why is it necessary and proper for Christ's apostles to suffer? (4:7-12)

5. What supports the apostles in their suffering and causes them not to lose heart? (4:13-18)

6. What final destiny do the apostles look forward to? (5:1-2)

7. What are the attitudes and activities of the apostles meanwhile? (5:2-9)

8. What effect does the apostles' knowledge of the coming Judgment have on the character of their ministry? (5:9-10)

Answer these questions by reading 2 Corinthians 5:11–6:13

9. What accusations against Paul and his colleagues does Paul refute in 5:12-13?

10. What motivates the ministry of Paul and his associates? (5:14-15)

11. What results from being "in Christ"? (5:16-21)

12. What has God done in Christ for the world? (5:19)

13. What is the function of the apostles in view of what God has done? (5:19-20)

14. What are the Corinthians to do in view of what God has done? (5:20b-6:2)

15. What are the marks of authenticity of true servants of God? (6:4-10)

DIMENSION TWO: WHAT DOES THE BIBLE MEAN?

■ **2 Corinthians 4:1-6.** Our ministry is overt (open, evident), not covert (concealed, secret), Paul says. Our ministry is founded on the principle of "setting forth the truth plainly" (4:2), the truth being set forth with confidence and even boldness (3:12). We have renounced the sort of "secret and shameful ways" (4:2) and crafty twisting of the truth (12:16) that our enemies at Corinth have used (2:17). Instead, we appeal directly to the conscience of the hearer under God's watchful eyes.

But not all who hear our gospel (good news) believe it. Why not? The gospel being "veiled" (hidden, concealed), as our enemies claim, is not the trouble, except to the "perishing" (4:3; "someone who is lost" [CEV]). The fact that they are not seeking and not understanding the truth is due to their unbelief and to the activity of Satan ("the god of this age"). Paul does not relieve hearers of their responsibility for positive response to the truth. Many are "unbelievers" (4:4). Because they do not believe, Satan has power to blind them.

Paul does not say that Satan blinded them so that they might not believe. The blinding follows their unbelief (2 Thessalonians 2:9-12), the appeal to their conscience having first been made (2 Corinthians 4:3).

Those who do believe see something marvelous to behold: "the glory of Christ, who is the image of God" (4:4).

Here glory is the brightness, radiance, and splendor that belong to God's Messiah, who is the exact image of God.

Paul goes on to say that we, God's true servants, lift up Jesus the Messiah as Lord; we do not lift up ourselves (4:5). God's glory shines in our hearts so that we may illuminate others with the glory of God that shines in Jesus Christ (4:6). To behold and to experience means to share!

■ **2 Corinthians 4:7-18.** To have God's glory in the heart and the privilege of sharing it through the gospel is a priceless treasure. The container for the treasure— "jars of clay," which God's servants are—is suited to God's purpose: namely, to reveal God's "all-surpassing" (incomparable) power and not to call attention to the human medium. Sophisticated, boastful, self-cultivated persons, strong and brilliant according to worldly standards, are enemies of the cross of Christ; relying on these attributes empties the cross of its power (1 Corinthians 1:17-29). Faith must not be anchored in the brilliance of humans but in the power of God (1 Corinthians 2:5).

A true apostle, therefore, is one who suffers and dies in weakness as the Lord did, so that God's resurrection power may be manifested (4:14). Those who do not suffer cannot be servants of a suffering Lord. While dying with Jesus (Paul sees Jesus' whole life as a dying, a dying he is duplicating), the true apostle shares in the resurrection life of Jesus. Thus the true apostle can glory in his or her weaknesses because God's power is experienced and revealed through weakness (2 Corinthians 12:9-10).

So God's suffering servants take heart in their sufferings. Their physical bodies are decaying and perishing as a result of their sufferings, but their inner selves are being renewed daily. Both death and life are at work within them, and both are preparing them for an eternal abundance of glory that will far outweigh the small and temporary sufferings they have endured in this life. Therefore, they keep their eyes on the unseen, eternal realities, not on things that belong to the passing, earthly scene.

■ **2 Corinthians 5:1-10.** Paul now pauses for a look at the eternal abundance of the apostles and believers. He contrasts our impermanent, tent-like existence on earth with the coming, eternal, building-like existence in heaven—in an order prepared by God, not by humans.

Paul raises the question of our attitudes and activities meanwhile. "We groan" (or sigh) in our longing for that new existence and the eternal spiritual body believers will have for life in that age. We are eager to be clothed with that body and to enter that new order.

Not that we actually long to die and depart this troublesome existence; but rather we long to obtain the fullness of that life that we received in anticipation (in down payment) through God's gift of the Holy Spirit to us.

In our groaning "we are always confident." While we are here in our earthly bodies and away from our final heavenly existence with the Lord, we walk in confident faith that our glorious future, not now present to our eyes, will be realized. We would prefer to be out of this body and "at home with the Lord"; but whether here or there, we aim to be pleasing to the Lord.

■ **2 Corinthians 5:11-21.** In the interval before the coming Judgment and the realization of our final and eternal existence in heaven, we, as God's servants, make it our aim to persuade people to be reconciled to God and to be ready to give account to God.

At this point, Paul gets defensive again. He has been accused of persuading people at Corinth and elsewhere by deceitful claims of apostolic authority, supported only by self-commendation, and of conducting his mission in insincere and crafty ways (1:12–2:2; 2:17–3:6; 5:12). He admits to the charge of being a persuader; but his persuading has been done only with God's full knowledge and by an appeal to the Corinthians' conscience, and in no other way. Paul wants his readers to be proud of him and to be able to answer the critics who judge him by outward, rather than inward, standards.

Paul turns aside the charge that he is emotionally unbalanced (or perhaps that he is using bizarre, ecstatic, psychic experiences to prove his apostleship) by asserting that any such ecstatic experiences were of a private nature—between him and God. His rational mind has been devoted to his ministry to the Corinthians.

In short, Paul says, we persuade people in sincerity because we are controlled by Christ's love. Christ's love led him to die on behalf of all persons so that all might die in identification with him and participate with him in the power of his resurrection. Being thus made alive, they no longer live selfish lives but live for him who gave himself in love for them.

As Paul's enemies have judged him according to outward human standards and thus misjudged him, so Paul once judged Jesus from these same standards. But no longer does he apply these human standards to Jesus. Paul sees that, through identification with Christ in his death and resurrection, a new age with transformed people has come into being. Everything old has come to an end, and new things have taken their place.

God, acting in Christ's death and resurrection for all humanity, brought about a reconciliation of estranged, sinful people of the world. The new age will have "righteousness" (5:21; that is, right relations with God and one another).

God gave us, says Paul, "the ministry of reconciliation" (5:18), and this ministry Paul immediately exercises on behalf of the estranged Corinthians: "We implore you on Christ's behalf: Be reconciled to God" (5:20).

■ **2 Corinthians 6:1-13.** The appeal in 6:1-10 is meant to move the Corinthians to reconciliation with Paul and his colleagues. He stresses the necessity and urgency of the Corinthians' fidelity to the gospel and its messengers (6:1-2) and again appeals to his authenticating credentials as an apostle: his sufferings for Christ. He is now ready for the direct appeal of 6:11-13.

DIMENSION THREE: WHAT DOES THE BIBLE MEAN TO ME?

2 Corinthians 4:2—Witness and the Conscience

For Paul, the conscience was the ability in a person to pass judgment on his or her own or others' attitudes and actions (1:12; Romans 2:15-16). He did not regard the conscience as so twisted by sin or mesmerized by demonic power (4:4) that it could not evaluate and act on the truth when forthrightly presented.

This should give us confidence in our witnessing. If God calls us, makes us adequate, and has confidence in the consciences of people to evaluate what we say—with no tricks or "human wisdom"—we too can be bold (3:12; can "not lose heart," 4:1, 16; "are . . . confident," 5:6, 8).

2 Corinthians 5:1-10—Faith, Not Sight

In this tent-like existence of longing for our permanent home, anxiety concerning our mortality, and separation from the Lord—a time of waiting for our glorious, building-like inheritance in heaven—we walk by faith, not by sight (5:7). But we do not walk in uncertainty, for we have the Spirit in our hearts "as a deposit" of our ultimate inheritance (5:5). This gives our faith "assurance" (Hebrews 11:1). We know by the Spirit within that we are "God's children" and "heirs" (Romans 8:14-17) and that nothing can separate us from our glorious future (Romans 8:35- 39). Knowing all this, it is our task to live a life pleasing to the Lord. In practical terms, what will this mean for you?

2 Corinthians 5:17-21—Reconciliation

One of the key words in Paul's vocabulary is *reconciliation*. That is what God, Christ, Paul, and the church are about in the world. In a fundamental sense, sin is alienation. Think about the areas of our lives in which alienation exists. What means are used in our secular society in the attempt to overcome alienation? How successful are they? What does Christianity offer as a means of reconciliation that these secular means do not offer? Describe the new creation (5:17) into which reconciliation brings us. Illustrate from your own life, if possible.

Thanks be to God for his indescribable gift! (9:15)

OPEN-HEARTED SHARING

2 Corinthians 6:14–9:15

DIMENSION ONE: WHAT DOES THE BIBLE SAY?

Answer these questions by reading 2 Corinthians 6:14–7:1

1. What is the central idea that binds this section together? (6:14–7:1)

2. What, if any, logical connection do you see between this section (6:14–7:1) and 6:11-13, on the one hand, and 7:2-3, on the other?

Answer these questions by reading 2 Corinthians 7:2-16

3. After reading this passage, what would you say Paul's mood was at the time of writing it? What words of his best describe this mood? (7:2-16)

4. What was the nature of Titus's news? (7:7b, 9, 11)

5. What was the effect of Paul's letter on himself and on the Corinthians? (7:8-9)

6. What was Paul's purpose in writing this letter? (7:12; 2:3-4, 9)

Answer these questions by reading 2 Corinthians 8:1–9:15

7. Why have the Macedonian churches given liberally to "this service to the Lord's people" (in Jerusalem)? (8:1-5)

8. Why should the church at Corinth give liberally to this project also? (8:6-15)

9. Whom is Paul sending to take up the offering at Corinth? (8:6, 16-23)

10. Why is Paul sending these men to Corinth in advance of his arrival? (9:3-5)

11. Why should the Corinthians give not only cheerfully but generously to this offering? (9:6-10)

12. What service to God will the Corinthians render by their generous giving? (9:11-13)

13. In what way will the Corinthians themselves be enriched by their giving? (9:11, 14)

14. In what way have God's and Christ's giving set the pattern for Christian giving? (8:1, 9; 9:8-10, 15)

DIMENSION TWO: WHAT DOES THE BIBLE MEAN?

Paul's catalog of his and his colleagues' sufferings as "servants of God" (6:4-10) sums up his argument in support of the authenticity of their apostolic ministry. He believes that the way is now cleared for a direct appeal to the Corinthians for reconciliation.

■ **2 Corinthians 6:14–7:1.** This passage fits awkwardly into its context. When you read 7:2 immediately after 6:13, the progress of thought is smooth and clear. It is not readily apparent why 6:14-7:1 is where it is.

Assuming that the passage is now where Paul originally placed it, what does it say to the Corinthians? The passage warns them that full reconciliation awaits their separation from intimate and defiling relationships with unbelievers. Since the Christian church is "the temple of the living God" (6:16), that temple must be a fit dwelling place for a holy God and God's cleansed sons and daughters. Defiling relationships with unbelievers will cancel out their future as God's children (7:1).

In a series of rhetorical questions (6:14-16) Paul suggests the incompatibility of good and evil, and he enforces his counsel against defiling relationships, quoting several scriptural passages. As God's people, the Corinthians are called to holiness of life (1 Corinthians 1:2; 6:11, 14-16).

■ **2 Corinthians 7:2-16.** Paul's plea for the Corinthians to open their hearts to him and his associates is not a request for them to share their inner thoughts and emotions but to receive him and his associates into their affections. The missionaries are not at fault for the strained relationship; on their side they are pledged to the Corinthians in an eternal relationship (7:3). As for Paul, he is now confident in, proud of, comforted by, and joyful over the Corinthians (7:4).

The rest of this passage (7:2-16) states three reasons for Paul's joy. First, he is joyful over the coming of Titus and the good report he brought about the Corinthians (7:5-7). After leaving Ephesus, Paul had expected to meet Titus at the city of Troas, but Titus was not there (2:12-13). So distraught was Paul in mind (2:13) and body (7:5) over Titus's failure that he could not continue his mission in Troas (2:12). Instead, he took ship to Macedonia, hoping to find Titus there, probably at Philippi.

At last Titus arrived, probably at Philippi, with joyful news. This news led Paul to write this letter (*Letter D*, see lesson 6). While, as we have seen, he still feels his apostolic position needs shoring up—which he proceeds to do in the first six chapters of this letter—the crisis in relationship is largely past (2:4-11). Paul can now express his relief and satisfaction to the Corinthians. They now long to see him; they mourn over their insulting attitudes and actions toward him, and they are once again zealous for him and his work (7:7).

Second, Paul is joyful over the good result of his painful letter (7:8-13a). This letter is lost (*Letter C*, see lesson 6). Paul also refers to it in 2:3-4, 9. This letter dealt with the Corinthian church's responsibility to discipline some persons who had insulted Paul (see page 53).

This letter must have been a "scorcher," one that Paul at first regretted having sent (7:8). But it produced results. The Corinthians' "sorrow led [them] to repentance" (7:9), as Titus seems to have found after he arrived. They are again zealous for Paul and his gospel (7:12). The case is closed, as far as Paul is concerned. And he states that "my joy knows no bounds" (7:4)!

Third, Paul is joyful over "how happy Titus was" (7:13b-15). Paul had praised the Corinthians to Titus. The Corinthians had vindicated Paul's confidence by their obedience to his (Paul's) instructions and by according Titus honor as Paul's representative. And they won Titus's respect and love (7:15). "I am glad" sums up the whole section (7:16).

■ **2 Corinthians 8:1-15.** In chapters 8 and 9, we find Paul's appeal for the Corinthians' support of the collection he has been taking up for the Jerusalem church.

Paul seems to have had several reasons for taking up this offering. First, the mother church had great need, a need Paul had earlier sought to meet when he was in Antioch (Acts 11:27-30). Christian love requires help from the churches with greater resources (8:9, 14).

Second, Paul believed that the offering would promote unity between the Jewish and the Gentile divisions of the church, perhaps wiping out deep-seated suspicion and hostilities between them and demonstrating the oneness of all in Jesus Christ (Galatians 3:28).

Third, the offering was both a fulfillment of the obligation Paul had accepted at the Jerusalem Conference (to "remember the poor," Galatians 2:10) and a tangible demonstration of the success of his work in the Gentile world—the field to which he had been assigned at that conference (Galatians 2:9).

Paul's way of motivating the Corinthians to give generously is noteworthy:

1. God's grace—working in the Macedonians, leading them to enthusiasm for the project and to great liberality, even in their affliction and poverty—has set the example for the Corinthians (8:1-5).

2. Titus, who made a beginning with the collection when he was in Corinth (and with whom the Corinthians have a good relationship, 7:13b-15), will return to complete "this act of grace" (8:6).

3. Since the Corinthians "excel in everything," they should excel in this also (8:7).

4. Paul is not commanding, but asking the Corinthians to prove, in comparison with the Macedonians, the genuineness of their love (8:8).

5. Paul is not commanding, but asking them to consider an appropriate response to the riches they received through the generosity of "our Lord Jesus Christ," who gave up his own riches to enrich us (8:9).

6. Paul is not commanding, but advising them to complete what they were willing to begin, even though they think the amount may not be as great as they would like (8:10-12).

7. The church needs to engage in mutual sharing and to make the care for one another equal; the Corinthians are giving now in the time of others' need and perhaps will receive from them in the future, with everyone's needs satisfied (8:13-15).

■ **2 Corinthians 8:16–9:5.** The second section of Paul's appeal for an offering from the Corinthians deals with the identity, the qualifications, and the function of the collectors Paul is sending to Corinth ahead of his arrival.

Titus is to head the delegation. Like Paul, he is solicitous for the well-being of the Corinthians and eager to return to Corinth to help with the project (8:16-17).

With Titus will come a famous preacher-messenger of certain (unnamed) churches, appointed by them to travel with Paul, to assist in the collection of the funds, and to insure the integrity of the operation. It appears from what Paul says here (8:20-21) that some persons at Corinth have questioned his motives in gathering "this liberal gift."

The delegation also will include a second (unnamed) brother, of tested devotion and deep confidence in the Corinthians (8:22).

All three are to be trusted: Titus as Paul's "partner and co-worker"; and the brothers as "representatives of the churches."

Paul explains in 9:1-5 why he is sending these persons ahead of his arrival at Corinth: so that the Corinthians' long-intended and publicized plan to contribute may come to fruition; so that Paul may not be embarrassed before Macedonian companions on his arrival at Corinth; and so that the money collected may appear as a "generous gift," not as something exacted by Paul himself (9:5).

■ **2 Corinthians 9:6-15.** The discussion of the collection ends with an appeal for generous and cheerful giving. The appeal is based on the law of the harvest and the generosity of God: bountiful sowing yields a bountiful harvest, and God gives generously so that recipients may be able to share generously. The consequences of bountiful giving for the giver are pointed out: enough for oneself (self-sufficiency), plenty of seed for sowing ("increase your store of seed"), and the opportunity to be greatly generous. *Righteousness* in 9:9-10 probably means "benevolence," as the footnote in the New Revised Standard Version suggests.

DIMENSION THREE: WHAT DOES THE BIBLE MEAN TO ME?

2 Corinthians 6:14–7:1—Believers and Unbelievers

Paul opposes the mis-mating (mis-yoking) of believers with unbelievers, though he does not advocate complete separation from them (1 Corinthians 5:9-10). How far should we apply this principle today in friendships, in marriage, in business relationships, in fraternal organizations, in recreation? Can we associate in intimate ways with unbelievers without becoming like them?

2 Corinthians 7:9-11—Godly Grief and Worldly Grief

Sorrow and grief can have two different effects on us. They can lead to self-pity, to cynicism about God and the world, and eventually to death (by suicide or attrition). Or they can lead to repentance and salvation. Judas Iscariot was sorry and took the world's way out—he took his own life (Matthew 27:3-5). Peter was sorry for his denial of Jesus ("he went outside and wept bitterly," Matthew 26:75), but his sorrow led him to repentance and salvation.

How can we explain the differing effects of sorrow? What difference do belief in the Christian God, the reality of sin, and the efficacy of prayer make?

2 Corinthians 8–9—Christian Sharing

Think about Paul's principles of giving, such as: we should give because God and Christ gave; we should give liberally because God will see that our needs will be supplied in excess; we should give cheerfully, even out of poverty; we should give in proportion to our means; giving will enrich the giver as well as the receiver; giving is an act of thanksgiving to God and will produce thanksgiving in those who receive our benevolence. What difference would it make in raising the church budget for projects at home and abroad if church members took Paul seriously? What difference would it make in your giving?

[The Lord] said to me, "My grace is sufficient for you, for my power is made perfect in weakness." (12:9)

APOSTLES: THE FALSE AND THE TRUE

2 Corinthians 10–13

DIMENSION ONE: WHAT DOES THE BIBLE SAY?

Answer these questions by reading 2 Corinthians 10

1. What charges does Paul refute in 10:1-6, and how?

2. How does Paul counter the claim and charge made in 10:7-11?

3. What does Paul object to in the attitude and activity of his rivals at Corinth? (10:12-18)

Answer these questions by reading 2 Corinthians 11:1-21a

4. Why is Paul jealous of the rivals who have come to Corinth? (11:2-6)

5. What problems arose between Paul and the Corinthians because he insisted on supporting himself while in Corinth? (11:7-11)

6. What estimate of Paul's rivals appears in 11:12-15?

7. In what ways have Paul's rivals ill-treated the Corinthians, and how have the Corinthians taken this treatment? (11:19-20)

Answer these questions by reading 2 Corinthians 11:21b–12:13

8. Why does Paul offer a catalog of his sufferings? (11:23-29)

9. How important as an apostolic credential does Paul think his experience of paradise was? (12:2-6)

10. What was the purpose of Paul's thorn in the flesh? (12:7-10)

11. What signs of a true apostle did Paul exhibit at Corinth? (12:12-13)

Answer these questions by reading 2 Corinthians 12:14–13:14

12. What accusation does Paul refute in 12:14-18?

13. What does Paul fear he will find when he arrives in Corinth? (12:20-21)

14. What does Paul want the Corinthians to do before he arrives? (13:5-9)

15. What is Paul's purpose in writing this letter? (13:10)

DIMENSION TWO: WHAT DOES THE BIBLE MEAN?

■ **2 Corinthians 10:1-18.** Paul's opponents at Corinth, whom he later calls "false apostles" (11:13) and "super-apostles" (11:5; 12:11), have poisoned the Corinthians' minds about Paul. He was aware of them when he wrote *Letter D* (2 Corinthians 1–9, see lesson 6), but his attack on them was mild (2 Corinthians 2:5-11; 2:17-3:1; 4:2; 5:12) in comparison to what he now has to say about them.

But they have also said hard things about Paul and forced him, against his will, to defend himself. They have said that he is humble, weak, and unimpressive in speech when present, and bold and autocratic in letters when absent (10:1, 9-11); that he lives "by the standards of this world" (10:2); that their relationship with Christ is superior to his (11:7); that he wants exclusive rights to the Corinthians, is too possessive of them, and boasts too much about his achievements (10:13-16).

Paul refutes each of these charges. It is the "humility and gentleness of Christ" that makes him humble (10:1), but he can be bold when present, if necessary (10:2, 6, 11). He lives in the world, but he does not fight with worldly weapons; he fights with all-conquering divine power, adequate to overthrow everything that opposes both the knowledge of God as revealed in the gospel and the lordship of Christ

(10:3-5). Paul gives no ground to those who claim to be closer to Christ than he is (10:7). He admits that he boasts "somewhat freely" about the authority the Lord gave him, but insists that it is for building up the Corinthians, not destroying them (10:8). He claims prior rights over the Corinthians on the ground that they fall within the territory God assigned him and were evangelized by him originally. Paul implies that his rivals are taking advantage of his labors in once virgin territory, poaching, as it were, in an area where he had staked out a claim, something that he has refused to do (10:15-16; Romans 15:20).

■ **2 Corinthians 11:1-21a.** In chapter 10, Paul criticizes his rivals for recommending themselves and comparing themselves with him to his disadvantage. He says he is against all self-recommendation and senseless, prideful comparisons (10:11- 12)—that all that matters is the Lord's commendation (10:18). If there is to be any boasting, one should "boast in the Lord" (10:17).

But now Paul indulges, contrary to his principle, in what one commentator has called "A Fool's Speech" (11:1–12:13). At the end of the speech, Paul says, "I have made a fool of myself, but you drove me to it" (12:11). It is evident from the rather embarrassed and lengthy introduction he makes to the speech (11:1- 2la) that he finds self-praise altogether obnoxious. He apologizes (11:1, 16-17) and tries to explain why he is doing such a thing. He cites the critical nature of the situation at Corinth that forces him to such foolish boasting.

The introduction makes several important points. Paul, the father of the virgin bride-to-be (the Corinthians), has betrothed her to Christ and is responsible for her chastity until the day of her marriage to him (at the Second Coming). But her purity and loyalty to bridegroom and father are threatened by other lovers (and Satan) to whom she seems ready enough to yield. The seductive lovers ("super-apostles") preach another Jesus, confer a different spirit, and advocate a different gospel on the ground that

GENESIS to REVELATION **2 CORINTHIANS**

they are superior to Paul, the father, in knowledge and speech. The inferiority in speech (Hellenistic rhetoric) Paul will admit, but not the inferiority in knowledge. There is no real reason for the bride-elect's rejection of her jealous (zealous) father's plans for her (11:2) and for her flirtation with other lovers.

In this introduction to the "Fool's Speech," Paul faces head-on a serious complaint by the Corinthians and probably the rival apostles about his dogged financial self-support. When he was at Corinth, he needed financial help. He accepted it from "other churches," from "brothers who came from Macedonia" (11:8-9), but made no claim on the Corinthians.

The Corinthians were offended by Paul's receiving support from others on several grounds: it seemed to imply a lack of love for the Corinthians on his part (11:11) and a preference for other churches; it contradicted normal Christian missionary practice, according to which missionaries accepted support for their labors (Matthew 10:9-10; 1 Corinthians 9:4, 6-14; 1 Timothy 5:17-18); they (and the people of the Hellenistic world) expected their philosophers and itinerant preachers to be compensated by their students, not to engage in demeaning manual work; and for them accepting gifts from benefactors brought social standing to the givers. Paul's attitude and practice seemed insulting to the Corinthians.

In defense, Paul says, somewhat sarcastically, that it was no "sin" (11:7), that he didn't want to "burden" the Corinthians (11:9), and that it was really an expression of his love for them (11:11). And he strongly implies that his rivals at Corinth are mercenary in attitude and practice and are exploiting the Corinthians (11:20). To Paul they are "deceitful workmen" and Satan's servants (11:13-15).

■ **2 Corinthians 11:21b–12:13.** In his speech, Paul boasts about several things: his credentials from heredity (11:22); his service (labors) for Christ (11:23-33); and his "visions and revelations" (12:1-10).

The rival teachers are proud of their Hebrew origin, that is, of their good breeding—a point much valued in the Hellenistic world. Paul equals them in this.

As to their labors for Christ, in no way can they compare with Paul's. The rival teachers apparently boast of their achievements, as Hellenistic and Roman heroes were wont to do. Paul, as a servant of Christ who suffered and was "crucified in weakness" (13:4), boasts rather of his sufferings and weaknesses. These are the signs of his true apostleship. Paul's achievements are failures from the world's point of view; and of these failures he will boast! He was a loser by popular standards, but a winner by God's.

The "false apostles" boast of their visions and revelations (and thus of their superior knowledge of God). Paul has had visions too (12:1-4)! He was caught up into paradise (in some experience otherwise unknown to us). But he did not understand his experience, learned nothing that he could communicate to others, and laid little store by this sort of thing.

The dramatic "signs, wonders and miracles," so valued by the Corinthians and the rival apostles as proof of apostleship, had occurred at Corinth as a result of Paul's ministry too (12:12), but he makes little of it.

The true apostle is one who suffers with the suffering Lord, serves Christ in absolute obedience, raises up and edifies his suffering and obedient church, and experiences with its members God's power in their common weakness (4:7-12)—not one who recounts achievements and who glories in "visions and revelations" and miraculous "signs."

■ **2 Corinthians 12:14—13:14.** The letter ends with an appeal for the Corinthians to prepare for Paul's third visit. He reaffirms his love for them, his innocence of their charges, and his desire to build up the church. He also shares his fears that they may not change and that he will have to deal strongly with them. They are to test themselves and mend their ways. Then, when he arrives, he can use his divinely given authority for constructive, rather than destructive, purposes.

DIMENSION THREE: WHAT DOES THE BIBLE MEAN TO ME?

2 Corinthians 10:1-6—The Power of Humility and Gentleness

Besides Jesus and Paul, what humble and gentle, yet powerful, people can you mention and describe? Consider their methods and the nature of their power, why it works and what kind of "strongholds" and "arguments" it destroys. Is it really true that the meek "will inherit the earth"? How widely do you think this is believed today?

2 Corinthians 10:13-18—"A Little Foolishness"

What is wrong with self-commendation? To succeed in anything, doesn't one need to "toot one's own horn" a bit? Is it only in Christian activities that boasting is inappropriate? And how about boasting about one's failures? What do you think of Plutarch's suggestion that self-praise is better received if one mentions also some personal flaw?[2] Is it true that one should boast only of the Lord (Jeremiah 9:23-24; 2 Corinthians 10:17)?

2 Corinthians 12:7-9—"A Thorn in [the] Flesh"

In bearing his "thorn in [the] flesh," Paul found God's abundant strength—strength that he would not have had without the thorn. People with disabling conditions have often found their disabilities to be assets. Can you illustrate this? What qualities of personality are needed to deal with disabilities? How can these qualities be developed? What part can dependence on God play in handling disabilities?

---

[2] See Frank Cole Babbitt, "On Praising Oneself Inoffensively" in *Plutarch's Moralia* (London: W. Heinemann; New York: G.P. Putnam, 1927), 109–168.

Does a thorn in the flesh come from God? Is it "a messenger of Satan" (12:7) or a biological or psychological quirk of nature? Did Paul believe that Satan could be an agent of God's purposes (Job 2:6-7; 1 Corinthians 5:5)? Do we need to know where a particular thorn comes from in order to deal creatively with it? Have you a thorn for which you thank God, even though you have to carry it?

*I have been crucified with Christ. . . . The life I live in the
body, I live by faith in the Son of God. (2:20)*

10

PAUL AND THE TRUE GOSPEL

Galatians 1–2; 6:11-18

DIMENSION ONE: WHAT DOES THE BIBLE SAY?

Answer these questions by reading Galatians (at one time, if possible); then reread chapter 1

1. What are the main ideas Paul is seeking to impress on the Galatians? (1:1, 11-12; 2:16, 19, 21; 5:1)

2. What differences do you find between the greeting in this letter and that in First Thessalonians? (1:1-5; 1 Thessalonians 1:1)

3. Compare the spirit in which Paul opens Galatians with his spirit in the opening verses of First Thessalonians. (1:6-10; 1 Thessalonians 1:2-10)

4. What does Paul tell us about his former life in Judaism? (1:13-14)

5. What does Paul tell us about his conversion experience? (1:15-16)

6. How much contact did Paul have with the Jerusalem apostles in the first few years after his conversion? (1:17-24)

Answer these questions by reading Galatians 2

7. What was Paul's purpose in going to Jerusalem the first time and the second time? (1:18; 2:2)

8. What part did Titus play in the second visit? (2:1-5)

9. What groups of people were present at this second visit? (2:1, 4, 9)

10. What agreement was reached between Paul and the Jerusalem apostles? (2:7-10)

11. Why did Paul oppose Peter (Cephas) at Antioch? (2:12-14)

12. How had both Paul and Peter been justified? (2:15-16)

13. What is the essence of Paul's rebuke of Peter? (2:17-20)

Answer these questions by reading Galatians 6:11-18

14. Who is actually writing here, and why do you think he takes the pen in his hand at this point? (6:11)

15. Why are the false teachers insisting that the Galatians be circumcised? (6:12-13)

16. What is Paul's attitude toward circumcision? (6:12-15)

17. What are "the marks of Jesus" that Paul bears on his body? (6:17; 2 Corinthians 11:23-25)

DIMENSION TWO: WHAT DOES THE BIBLE MEAN?

Many people agree that Galatians is the Magna Carta of Christian freedom and the charter of evangelical faith. Through this letter and that to the Romans, Paul has profoundly affected the course of Christian history and theology.

We have a little information about Paul's opponents in Galatia. They are hostile to Paul's claim to be an apostle of Jesus Christ and assert that his apostleship has only a human, not a divine, origin (1:1, 12). They believe Paul is self-appointed, seeking "the approval of human beings" (1:10), and received all that he knows about the gospel from human teachers, such as the Jerusalem apostles (1:16-19). They hold that his version of the gospel—that faith in Christ crucified is the only requirement for salvation for both Jews and Gentiles; that the Mosaic covenant with its requirements has been fulfilled and annulled by Christ's saving work (3:23-28)—is false. They assert that covenant and its laws are still binding on disciples of Jesus: both Jews and Gentiles must be circumcised (6:12-13), observe the sabbath and the festivals of the Jewish calendar (4:10), and keep separate from uncircumcised Gentiles (2:11-14).

By showing that they are good Jews, as well as Christians, these opponents think they and their followers will avoid persecution by Jews who object to the idea that the cross of Christ as the way of salvation has annulled the Mosaic covenant and its requirements (5:11; 6:12, 14).

The opponents seem also to have objected to Paul's teaching about freedom in Christ and the Spirit, on the ground that it promotes immoral living (5:13, 16). But they themselves do not keep the law, Paul says (6:13), implying perhaps that they are hypocritical or selective in what laws they keep. Their zeal for circumcision is more to make a good showing outwardly than it is zeal for the law itself (6:12).

We probably shall not be far wrong in saying that the opponents are Judaizing Jewish Christians from Jerusalem or endorsed by the legalistic Christian group there (2:4), who are intent on overturning Paul's law-free gospel and work among the Gentiles.

■ **Galatians 1:1-5.** This greeting, like the one in the Letter to the Romans, is far from routine. It shapes the traditional Hellenistic pattern (writer to recipients: greetings) in such a way as to affirm the main argument of the letter from the very start.

The greeting contains three elements: a statement concerning Paul's authority (an apostle by divine appointment, 1:1); a statement concerning his message (the gospel of God's redeeming grace in Christ crucified and risen, 1:1, 3-4); and an expression of Paul's attitude toward what God has done (Christ's redemption is sufficient and adequate, thank God! 1:5).

■ **Galatians 1:6-10.** Paul omits the thanksgiving, normal here in Hellenistic letters and in his own, and immediately plunges into his reason for writing. He is astonished at the

Galatians' speedy desertion from God, who has called them into the state of grace in which they now stand, and at their turn to a different gospel, which is not just another version of the true gospel (1:6-7).

Paul then affirms the absolute truth and finality of the gospel he had preached to them. He twice pronounces a curse on anyone, even himself or an angel from heaven, who would advocate a gospel contrary to his (1:8-9).

At the end of the letter (6:16), Paul pronounces a blessing on those who are the true people of God (6:14). The letter thus has a double aspect: a curse on those who oppose salvation through Jesus Christ alone and a blessing on those who accept it.

■ **Galatians 1:11-24.** This section begins a statement of facts about Paul's life that have a bearing on the truth or falsity of his divine authority and of his gospel. The statement continues to 2:14, at which point the issue to be argued in the rest of the letter is summarized (2:15-20).

First, Paul shows that his conversion from Judaism and its accompanying special revelation of the true nature of the gospel were acts of God, independent of human mediation (1:11-16b).

Next, Paul shows that his independent missionary activity and his virtual lack of contact with the apostles of Jesus and the churches of Judea prove that God, not other people, is directing his activity.

■ **Galatians 2:1-10.** Paul went to Jerusalem at divine direction (2:2). He implies that it was not because he was sent as a delegate from Antioch (Acts 15:2-3), was summoned there to give an account of himself, or was a humble petitioner needing guidance. Paul pressed his case and won the leaders' approval over the objections of "false believers," who insisted on the acceptance of circumcision and the whole Jewish law by Gentiles. The leaders did not require the circumcision of the Gentile Titus, positively endorsed Paul's law-free ministry to the Gentiles, assigned the Gentile field to his authority, and asked only that he help the poor in Jerusalem. All this was a victory for Paul's divinely given gospel.

■ **Galatians 2:11-14.** The conference in Jerusalem had not ruled on whether or not *Jewish* Christians must continue to obey the dietary and purity laws of Judaism, which, among other things, forbade eating with Gentiles.

When Cephas (Aramaic equivalent of Peter) came to Antioch, he must have assumed that the decisions of the Jerusalem Conference meant that Gentile (uncircumcised) Christians were to be treated as full members of the same body as Jewish Christians; so he ate with them in free and open fellowship. The arrival of a conservative (legalistic) delegation from James, the Lord's brother and head of the Jerusalem church, brought a challenge to Peter's practice on the ground that the Jerusalem Conference exempted only Gentiles, not Jews, from Jewish law. As a result, Peter, Barnabas, and other Jewish Christians withdrew from table fellowship with the Gentile Christians.

Paul was horrified by their insincerity and inconsistency. Actually, Peter was putting pressure on the Gentile Christians to accept the law as a means of achieving fellowship and unity in the church—an intolerable betrayal in light of the decisions of the Jerusalem Conference and Paul's own divinely given gospel!

Paul tells the story here for several reasons: to show the independence of his authority and his gospel from human control (1:1, 11-12)—even from the honored Peter, to whom, it was alleged by his enemies, he was indebted (1:18); to offer a historical parallel to the present Galatian situation of pressure from the same Jewish-Christian legalists for Gentile-Christian observance of the Jewish law; and to set the stage for his rebuttal of the legalistic position in chapters 3 and 4.

■ **Galatians 2:15-21.** The issue to be debated is set forth here. Does anyone (Jew or Gentile) need to obey the law to be justified (put in right relation) with God now and at the Final Judgment? Both Peter and Paul, as Jews by birth, said no when they became Christians. They abandoned the way of law ("died to the law," 2:19) and instead put their faith in Jesus as the way of justification. To go back on this commitment—as Peter did and the Galatians are doing—is to "set aside the grace of God" and make Christ's death pointless.

DIMENSION THREE: WHAT DOES THE BIBLE MEAN TO ME?

Galatians 1:1-11—God's Gospel and Our Gospel

What contemporary philosophies or religions can you mention that seem designed to please humans and not God? How many of these are "do-it-yourself" philosophies or religions? What, according to Paul, pleases God?

Galatians 1:12-16—Paul's Conversion

Though Paul does not mention it here, was he prepared in any way for this experience? What was the heart of the experience? From what was Paul converted and to what? Is his experience altogether unique? Has anything like this happened to you or others you know? What should we think of more gradual conversions?

Galatians 2:11-14—Peer Pressure

How are convictions formed? How can we know that they are right? Must we always stand firmly by them, or is compromise or abandonment sometimes proper? What kinds of considerations should motivate change in convictions? What can we do when neither to "stand pat" nor to give in seems right? What resources for supporting our convictions are available to us?

It is for freedom that Christ has set us free. . . . But do not use your freedom to indulge the flesh. (5:1, 13)

11

FREEDOM IN CHRIST AND THE SPIRIT

Galatians 3:1–6:10

DIMENSION ONE: WHAT DOES THE BIBLE SAY?

Answer these questions by reading Galatians 3

1. What arguments from the Galatians' personal experience does Paul present to support his thesis that justification is by faith alone? (3:1-5)

2. How do Abraham's experience and expectation, as revealed in Scripture, support this thesis? (3:6-9)

3. How does Scripture further prove the thesis? (3:10-14)

4. How does common legal practice confirm the thesis? (3:15-18)

5. What was God's purpose in giving the law? (3:19-24)

6. What results have come about through faith in Christ Jesus? (3:25-29)

Answer these questions by reading Galatians 4

7. How does the law concerning inheritance support the thesis, and how are the Galatians violating the principle involved here? (4:1-11)

8. What appeal does Paul make on the basis of his personal relationship with the Galatians? (4:12-20)

9. How does the law testify against itself as the way of salvation? (4:21-31)

Answer these questions by reading Galatians 5:1–6:10

10. What reasons does Paul give for his appeal to the Galatians not to become circumcised? (5:1-6)

11. What have Paul's enemies in Galatia done to the Galatians and to Paul? (5:7-11)

12. What problem may result from the Galatians' freedom in Christ? (5:13, 16-17)

13. What suggestions has Paul for dealing with a Christian caught in sin? (6:1-2)

14. What warning against spiritual pride does Paul give? (6:3-5)

15. What is Paul trying to teach by the analogy of sowing and reaping? (6:7-10)

DIMENSION TWO: WHAT DOES THE BIBLE MEAN?

Chapters 3 and 4 present Paul's proofs that justification is by faith alone and not by obedience to the Jewish law.

■ **Galatians 3:1-5.** First, Paul offers an argument from the Galatians' own experience. Paul's dramatic portrayal of Jesus Christ crucified had led to their acceptance of Christ by faith and to the reception of the Spirit and miracle-working power into their lives. They had begun well in their life of faith (trust) in Christ and in their experience of the Spirit. Paul asks why they are so foolish as to think that they can come to Christian maturity on a different path than that on which they began? "Trying to finish by means of the flesh" (3:3) is a reference to their acceptance (or contemplated acceptance) of circumcision (6:12). Keep on in faith and in the Spirit, Paul says.

■ **Galatians 3:6-14.** Paul continues with an argument from Scripture. He starts with Abraham, whom the false teachers of Galatia apparently used as proof that circumcision was necessary for inclusion in the family of Abraham and for inheriting the blessing God promised to him (Genesis 17).

Paul turns their argument around and shows that Abraham's relationship with God (Abraham's "righteousness") rested on his belief in God (Genesis 15:6), rather than on his acceptance for himself and his family of the rite of circumcision. Thus, the essential mark of the children of Abraham is faith in God, not fleshly circumcision; and uncircumcised Gentiles who have faith like Abraham's are also God's true children and heirs.

The Scripture testifies that seeking a right relationship with God by obedience to the Jewish law (including circumcision) leads to condemnation by the law. The law demands perfect obedience (something that no one can do) and curses those who fail. Even the attempt is misguided, because the Scripture says that "the righteous will live by faith" (3:11; Habakkuk 2:4), and that salvation by obedience to the law is salvation by works, not by faith (Leviticus 18:5).

Jews under the law are under a curse, and any Gentiles who accept the law as the way of salvation will likewise suffer the curse. Escape from the curse comes only by faith in Jesus Christ. As God's Son, Jesus became man ("born of a woman") and came under the curse of the law ("born under law") "to redeem those under law" in order that we might become children of God along with him (4:4-5). How Jesus bought out cursed humanity is not explained here, but simply affirmed.

Since salvation is by faith in God's deed in Christ, it is open to Gentiles who have faith.

■ **Galatians 3:15–4:7.** Arguing from contemporary legal practice, Paul now says that God's covenant of promise-faith with Abraham preceded the Mosaic law by 430 years and is not annulled or modified by that law. Its terms, as originally given, will surely be carried out with Abraham's offspring ("Christ" and those who have faith in him).

The Mosaic law was introduced to deal somehow with human sin (3:19, 22) and was designed to have only a temporary role until the coming of Christ and salvation by faith.

What the role of the law is, Paul brings out through an analogy. The Jews before Christ were like children under "supervision guardian." A guardian was not a teacher but a slave, who accompanied an underage heir (always a boy) to and from school, warded off dangers, carried his school supplies, and disciplined him when necessary. When the boy became of age, the guardian was no longer needed.

The law was an arrangement for guiding and disciplining immature and sinful people. It put under a curse those who did not and could not obey it perfectly, and provided no way to escape from its curse. By a perverse sort of negative stimulation (people often want to do what is prohibited), the law multiplied transgressions and made the human situation worse. The law brought knowledge of sin but no power to overcome it. This power comes through faith in Christ (Romans 7:24-25; Galatians 3:13; 4:4-7).

■ **Galatians 4:8-20.** The Jews are in slavery under the law, and the Gentiles are in bondage to "the weak and miserable principles" (4:9; also see 4:3). These principles or spirits seem to be in part astral spirits, ruling the heavenly bodies, the calendar and festivals derived from these bodies (Galatians 4:10), and dictating regulations concerning conduct (Colossians 2:20-21). Christ came to destroy these demonic spirits and set people free. For the Galatians to go under the law is the same as to go back to bondage under false spirits.

In 4:12-20, Paul gives up formal argument and makes a strong personal appeal to the Galatians: once, they shared mutual acceptance and love with Paul. The nature of his ailment, which did not turn them away from him, is not stated, though it probably was the "thorn in my flesh," mentioned in 2 Corinthians 12:7.

■ **Galatians 4:21-31.** Paul's allegory (actually allegory and typology mixed) concerning Hagar-Ishmael-the Jews-the earthly Jerusalem, on the one hand, and Sarah-Isaac-the Christians-the heavenly Jerusalem, on the other, must have infuriated any Jews who were told of Paul's views. The contrast here reduces Judaism to a kind of bastard Ishmaelite status and predicts its rejection by God (4:30).

Allegory sees meanings in the details of a story that are not evident on the surface. *Typology* sees anticipation of

New Testament persons, events, institutions, and truths in the Old Testament, and holds that the Old Testament anticipations are fulfilled in the new. Paul frequently used typology (1 Corinthians 5:7; 10:1-11), as did other Christian writers (Hebrews 3:7-4:11; 1 Peter 3:21).

■ **Galatians 5:1–6:10.** This section deals with the nature of Christian freedom. Paul has shown that Christ came to set people free from the bondage of the law and of the demonic powers. He is distressed and almost angry that the Galatians would consider returning to the bondage offered them by the false teachers. Note his explosion in 5:12, where he calls on the "agitators" to "go the whole way and emasculate themselves!"

Paul says clearly that to accept circumcision and to go under the law as a way of salvation is to cut oneself off from Christ. It is to fall away from the way of faith-grace and from life in the Spirit. The false teachers are making too much of circumcision. All that is important is "faith expressing itself through love" (5:6), or, as Paul puts it later, "a new creation" (6:15). If we have faith that is active in loving attitudes and deeds, we are "a new creation," creatures of the new age that came with Christ. How can one go back to the old age and its bondage?

Freedom is God's intention for life in the new age (5:13). This freedom is not to be used "to indulge the flesh." This freedom is controlled by love and service of one's neighbor and by the source of that love, the Holy Spirit. If we live by the Spirit's presence, power, and guidance, we will enjoy and manifest the Spirit's fruit (5:22-23) in our freedom. We will not follow the dictates of our lower self into a life of evil attitudes and acts (5:19-21).

Finally, Paul shows the meaning of love in relation to those who fall into sin (6:1-5) and those who teach "the word" to the Galatians (6:6): forgiving, nonjudgmental restoration, and helpfulness to the student and sharing "all good things" with the teacher.

The section ends with a warning and a promise. Those who live a sinful, fleshly life will reap a harvest of "destruction." Those who live a Spirit-filled and Spirit-controlled life will reap "eternal life." Such a life will mean doing good to all people, especially to fellow Christians.

DIMENSION THREE: WHAT DOES THE BIBLE MEAN TO ME?

Galatians 3:10-14—Law and Grace

What is the effect of law (civil and moral law) on you? Does it help you toward better living and personal righteousness, or does it frustrate you? Has law any function in the promotion of Christian living?

Galatians 4:3-10—The Demonic Powers

Many people have considered belief in demons and Satan a piece of ancient mythology that modern people can well do without. Is our life actually in bondage to forces that we cannot control? Are we in need of divine help to deliver us from our bondage to those forces? What might some of these forces be? One scholar mentions "the current climate of opinion" as one of these. Suggest some others, and examine how they operate on you and other people. How have you gained victory over them?

Galatians 5:13-26—Christian Freedom

What is Christian freedom? Paul insists that Christians are free, yet in the same breath calls for them to "serve one another humbly in love" (5:13). Paul was a slave to his mission and his churches, carrying unbelievably heavy burdens for them (2 Corinthians 11:28). What responsibilities does Christian freedom involve for you? What liberties does that freedom allow you? What controls on these liberties do you believe you have?

He made known to us the mystery of his will according to his good pleasure, which he purposed in Christ, to be put into effect when the times reach their fulfillment—to bring unity to all things in heaven and on earth under Christ. (1:9-10)

12

THE DIVINE PLAN

Ephesians 1–3

DIMENSION ONE: WHAT DOES THE BIBLE SAY?

Answer these questions by reading Ephesians 1

1. For what is God praised in 1:3-6?

2. For what is Christ praised in 1:7-12?

3. For what is the Holy Spirit praised in 1:13-14?

4. Who is meant by *us*, *we*, and *you*? (1:3-14)

5. How well does Paul know the readers of this letter? (1:15; see also 3:2)

6. For what about the readers does Paul give thanks? (1:15-16)

7. When Paul prays for the readers, what does he ask of God for them? (1:17-19)

8. What evidence of the greatness of God's power does Paul give? (1:20-23)

Answer these questions by reading Ephesians 2

9. Describe the condition in their former life of the persons designated as *you* and *we*. (2:1-3, 11-16)

10. How did the great change in *you* and *us* occur? (2:4-5, 8-9, 13, 17)

11. What privileges (present and future) are there for those who have been brought together by Christ? (2:6-7, 13-16, 18, 19-22)

Answer these questions by reading Ephesians 3

12. What is the content of the "mystery of Christ" that was made known to Paul and the holy apostles and prophets? (3:4-6)

13. What is Paul's role in relation to this mystery? (3:7-9)

14. What is the role of the church in relation to the mystery? (3:10)

15. What does Paul ask God to grant to the readers of this epistle? (3:16-19)

16. How great is God's power in the Christian? (3:20)

DIMENSION TWO: WHAT DOES THE BIBLE MEAN?

This letter is really a treatise about the church: its divine origin, its racial components, its mission and function in the universe, its destiny as the people of God, its apostolic leadership, and the privileges and responsibilities of its members. The theme of Ephesians may be stated thus: It is God's purpose to unite the universe in Christ and the church.

In Paul's time, deep divisions fragmented human life. He calls attention to some of them: Jew and Greek, slave and free, male and female, circumcised and uncircumcised, Greeks and barbarians, the wise and foolish (Romans 1:14; Galatians 3:28; Colossians 3:11). Moreover, division is seen in the heavenly sphere also: God, Christ, and the Holy Spirit against "all rule and authority, power and dominion" (Ephesians 1:21), "the ruler of the kingdom of the air" (2:2), "the rulers and authorities in the heavenly realms" (3:10), "the powers of this dark world and . . . the spiritual forces of evil in the heavenly realms (6:12), and "the devil" (6:11). Paul sees God's purpose to be the elimination, through Christ and the church, of discordant and hostile division everywhere and the creation of universal unity and peace.

In a deeply divided world like ours, Ephesians sings triumphantly to us about the victory of God and the church (accomplished and promised) over the powers of chaos that threaten to engulf us. It gives us strength to go on believing that Christ "is our peace," that he has "destroyed the barrier, the dividing wall of hostility," and that he is creating a new society of reconciled people in eternal fellowship with one another and God (2:14-22).

■ **Ephesians 1:1-2.** Many scholars today believe that Ephesians was written by a follower of Paul and in Paul's name, somewhat later than Paul's life (between about AD 80 and 95) in order to bring Paul's insights about the church to bear on problems of the writer's time. Where this person lived can only be conjectured (possibly Ephesus or elsewhere in Asia Minor).

However, equally good scholars defend Paul's authorship and regard this letter as his most mature work. Written while he was a prisoner (3:1; 4:1), when he had time to meditate about the significance of the church as a whole, Paul wrote a treatise for the entire church: to advance its reconciling mission in the earth, and to promote the internal health and unity of its members, who were to carry out that reconciling mission. These scholars most commonly place its writing in Rome, about AD 61–63, although some hold that Ephesus around AD 55 is possible.

The epistle probably was not addressed to the Ephesian church, though a copy of it may have been found there. The words in Ephesus do not appear in the oldest Greek manuscript of Ephesians and are missing from other important early manuscripts. No personal greetings to people whom Paul knew intimately through a long stay at Ephesus are given, and no problems unique to that church are discussed—only those common to all the churches founded by Paul. Copies of this letter may have been sent to various churches, or one copy may have circulated widely at first.

■ **Ephesians 1:3-14.** The magnificent blessing with which the epistle opens (in the Greek text, comprising one long sentence from 1:3 to 1:14) sets forth the theme of the entire document. The blessing is a poem of praise to God, to Christ, and to the Holy Spirit for beginning, accomplishing, and guaranteeing the plan for uniting the universe through the church (1:9-10).

■ **Ephesians 1:15-23.** The blessing is followed by a thanksgiving and prayers for the readers, of whose faith and love the writer has only "heard" (1:15; see also 3:2-3; 4:21).

Prayers for them include the following points: (1) that they may possess the Spirit who gives understanding and experience of God; and (2) that they may grasp in their innermost being the hope God's call holds for them, the richness of the glorious inheritance God has planned for the saints, and how great God's power at work in them really is.

■ **Ephesians 2.** This chapter shows how the divine plan for the unifying of all things and its implementing power is working out on the earthly plane. The power that worked mightily in Christ has been and now is at work in *us* (Jewish Christians) and in *you* (Gentile Christians).

The divine power has achieved a double result: resurrection from the dead of Jews and Gentiles with Christ (2:1-10), and reconciliation of Jews and Gentiles with God and with one another through Christ's sacrificial death (2:11-22). Both sections show contrast between what was and what now is, and include a declaration about how the change came about.

The spiritual death that characterized the former life of both Jewish and Gentile Christians was a disobedient, sinful, sensuous way of life under the sway of the evil power that rules this age and manifests in evil people. They were objects of God's wrath, like sinful humanity as a whole.

But the merciful, gracious, loving God raised them together with Christ from this condition of death into a heavenly existence of fellowship with God, with its certainty of ultimate enrichment.

This transformation occurred as a result of God's undeserved favor ("grace") and their response of trust ("faith"). It was a gift from God, not something they achieved by their own effort and of which they might boast (2:10).

The alienation and hostility between Gentiles and Jews and between both of them and God, which was overcome in Christ, is treated next. Uncircumcised Gentiles were separated from the Messiah (Christ), from the community of Israel, from the covenants that contained promises and hope for the future, and from God. They were once "far away" (2:17).

But, in the sacrificial death of Christ Jesus, the separated Gentiles have been brought into union with Christ and with Christian Jews. He has made peace between them by making them one people. Christ Jesus abolished the chief obstacle separating them and causing hostility between them: the (Jewish) law with its commandments and ordinances. Christ is the embodiment of peace. Through their incorporation in him, they have become one new person (humanity or people), and now have intimate access to God, as children have to a parent; one Spirit joins them to one another and to God.

The chapter ends (2:19-22) with three metaphors: political, domestic, and religious. The Gentile Christians are no longer "foreigners and strangers" (without the rights of citizenship) but are citizens along with "God's people." They are also family members in God's house (not outsiders looking in). And they are stones in the temple of God, built on the foundation stones of apostles and prophets, with Christ as the cornerstone—the whole growing structure the dwelling place of God's Spirit.

■ **Ephesians 3.** Chapter 2 has shown that Christ is the unifier of Jews and Gentiles. Chapter 3 affirms that Paul is the apostle sent out by God to preach to the world the unity that is being achieved in Christ. At the end of the chapter (3:14-19) the apostle of unity prays for the church: that it may have deep spiritual experience and the ability to comprehend the purpose of God for which it exists. An outburst of praise in a stately doxology (3:20-21) ends the chapter and the first half of Ephesians.

The chapter begins with an incomplete sentence (3:1) and a grammatical digression (though not a logical digression), running from verse 2 to verse 13. Paul apparently intended to pray here for the readers, as he does in verse 14, but instead broke off to explain why he was "a prisoner of Christ Jesus for the sake of you Gentiles." Logically this place would be right for him to explain his mission in relation to God's program of unification.

Paul assumes that his readers have heard of God's gracious gift to him of the good news concerning the inclusion of the Gentiles in God's plan of salvation. God gave Paul this knowledge as a special privilege not accorded people of other generations. Though the "mystery" was known by other Christians, it was Paul's particular commission to be a "servant" (3:7) of this gospel and to take it to the Gentile world. Though Paul was altogether unworthy of this high commission and privilege, God graciously appointed him to preach to the Gentiles "the boundless riches of Christ" in the long-hidden plan of God, the Creator. The church formed by this Messiah has a cosmic as well as an earthly role: to reveal to the (evil) spiritual powers that their days are numbered and that sovereignty in the future belongs to Christ and the church. Paul's suffering (imprisonment) in such a great ministry on behalf of the Gentiles should cause the readers to rejoice, rather than to be discouraged.

The prayer of 3:14-19, represented as offered from a kneeling or prostrate position and, therefore, of unusual emotion and earnestness, contains petitions for several needs of the readers: inner strength through the indwelling Spirit and the indwelling Christ; steadfastness in love, a love like the unfathomable love of Christ; the ability to comprehend with all God's people the immensity of God's and Christ's loving plan for the universe (see 1:18); and the attaining of the fullness (completeness) of being God intends for them.

The doxology praises the God who, working in us (by the Spirit), can do infinitely more than we can ask or conceive and celebrates his glory as manifested in the church and in Christ Jesus.

DIMENSION THREE: WHAT DOES THE BIBLE MEAN TO ME?

Ephesians 1:9-10—The Divine Plan

This epistle teaches that God is working out a purpose in human history. Many people see no purpose in the events of human life on this planet. How would Paul respond to these people?

Ephesians 2:13-17—The Peace-Bringer

Jesus Christ and the church, which is his "body" (1:23), are represented in Ephesians as God's means of reconciling the discordant elements of the created universe. What evidence is there that any unification has been or is being achieved through the coming of Christ and the church into the world?

Ephesians 3:14-19—The Complete Christian

What is Paul's picture of the complete Christian, according to this prayer? How do you—and how can you—measure up to it?

Make every effort to keep the unity of the Spirit through the bond of peace. (4:3)

THE PATH TO UNITY

Ephesians 4–6

DIMENSION ONE: WHAT DOES THE BIBLE SAY?

Answer these questions by reading Ephesians 4:1-16

1. What qualities of spirit contribute toward unity in the church? (4:2-3)

2. What unities already exist? (4:4-6)

3. What gifts has Christ bestowed on the church, and why were they given? (4:11-13)

Answer these questions by reading Ephesians 4:17–5:20

4. What attitudes and practices belong to the old nature? (4:17-22)

5. What is the new nature like? (4:23-24)?

6. What specific antisocial attitudes and practices of the old life should be abandoned? (4:25-32)

7. What new attitudes and practices should take their place? (4:25-32)

8. What attitudes and practices belong to the old darkness of pagan life? (5:3-18)

9. What attitudes and practices should characterize the "children of light"? (5:3-20)

Answer these questions by reading Ephesians 5:21–6:9

10. To what relationship is the Christian husband-wife relation compared? (5:21-33)

11. What is the standard for the husband's love of his wife? (5:25, 28-29, 33)

12. What reasons does Paul offer for children's obedience to their parents? (6:1-4)

Answer these questions by reading Ephesians 6:10-20

13. What is the posture of the Christian in the battle with the forces of evil? (6:11, 13, 14)

14. What aggressive attitudes and activities should the Christian warrior assume? (6:15, 17-20)

DIMENSION TWO: WHAT DOES THE BIBLE MEAN?

After the great song of praise for God's plan and its accomplishment in the unification of Jews and Gentiles through the mission of God's apostle, and after prayers for the readers' understanding of the plan, Paul turns to the implication of the plan for daily living. The "then" or "therefore" (NRSV) of 4:1 indicates that inferences are being drawn from what has preceded.

Paul's method throughout his letters is, as scholars put it, to follow his indicatives with imperatives: since in Christ you are thus and so, you must become and do thus and so. For example, he says: "Since we live by the Spirit, let us keep in step with the Spirit" (Galatians 5:25); and "Get rid of the old yeast, so that you may be a new unleavened batch—as you really are" (1 Corinthians 5:7). In some letters, the largely indicative beginning is followed by an imperative ending, thus dividing the letters into well-marked sections. This is clearly the case: chapters 1–3 praise what the church is; chapters 4–6 point out what, in the light of this information, the church should be and do.

But it is not only method, it is sound theology. Before God makes demands of us, God transforms us through grace and empowers us by the gift of the Holy Spirit. Then and then only are we able to begin to fulfill God's requirements.

■ **Ephesians 4:1-16.** Paul's reference to his present state as "a prisoner for the Lord" highlights his right to speak for the Lord, since suffering for the Lord is the true mark of authenticity as an apostle (2 Corinthians 4:7-12; 6:4-10; 11:23-29). He is asking, not for sympathy, but for attentive hearing and obedience.

How is the unity, conceived in the mind of God before the creation of the world (1:4-5, 9-10), to be implemented on the plane of history and consummated in the age to come (1:11; 5:5)?

First, church members are to have the attitudes that promote and maintain unity (4:2-3).

These attitudes include being "humble" (humility—disdained by the Greeks but exalted and demonstrated by Jesus [Mark 10:42-45; Philippians 2:5-8]); "gentle" (unassuming gentleness—the opposite of self-assertiveness—also disdained by the Greeks but embodied by Jesus [Matthew 11:29]); "patient" (forbearance in non-retaliation, manifested by Jesus [1 Peter 2:20-23]); "bearing with one another in love" (this love is the human response to, and extension of, God's and Christ's love [1:5; 2:4; 3:19; 5:2, 25; 6:23]); and making "every effort to keep the unity of the Spirit through the bond of peace."

Second, the members should contemplate and emphasize the unities they already possess and confess (4:4-6).

Seven unities are given: "one body" (one church incorporating diverse peoples made into one [2:14]); "one Spirit" (who seals Christians, inhabits the church as its temple, and reveals God's secret to the apostles and prophets [1:13; 2:22; 3:5]); "one hope" (of inheriting God's riches [1:18]); "one Lord" (Jesus Christ, "the Beloved" [1:5-6]); "one faith" (trust in Christ and loyalty to him, probably not one body of doctrine [2:8]); "one baptism" (one water rite at the time of incorporation into the church [Romans 6:3-4; 1 Corinthians 12:13]); "one God and Father of all" (the creator, permeator, and indweller of all things [see 3:14,15; 1 Corinthians 8:6]). With so many unities before it, the church should grow in unity (4:15-16).

Third, the church should use its Christ-given diversity for the promotion of unity (4:7-16).

The God of this epistle is a God who gives richly: God graciously gave the Messiah as the Redeemer (1:6-8; 2:4-5), and through the Messiah, God graciously bestows gifts on every believer (4:7).

That the Messiah, victorious over his enemies (the powers and authorities), is the source of the church's many gifts is proved by Scripture (Psalm 68:18), says Paul. He is "the LORD" (Psalm 68:17) who, after descending to the earth (the underworld, perhaps referring to Sheol), ascended on high, and, out of his largess, distributes gifts.

The gifts listed here are persons in differing forms of ministry: apostles, prophets, evangelists, pastors, teachers. Paul speaks in 1 Corinthians 12:4-11 as if the gifts are aptitudes or abilities; but, since these are present in persons, the distinction offers little difference (see also 1 Corinthians 12:28). Charismatic diversity at Corinth gave rise to divisiveness, which Paul tried to overcome with the analogy of the human body. So here he points out that the diverse gifts are meant to promote growth, health, and unity in the body of Christ. Use them in this way, he seems to say.

■ **Ephesians 4:17–5:20.** In this section, a fourth way of implementing God's purpose of unifying the cosmos is set forth: the church—the children of God and heirs of God's promised future—is to demonstrate in its personal and corporate life the quality of life of the age to come ("the kingdom of Christ and of God" [Ephesians 5:5]).

Continuing with old pagan attitudes and practices is even more destructive of unity in the church than competitive use of gifts. In two series of contrasts, separated by a summarizing and introductory admonition (5:1-2), Paul urges his readers to become in actuality what they are ideally. By wrong attitudes and actions, the Holy Spirit, who has "sealed" believers "for the day of redemption," can be grieved and offended (4:30), jeopardizing their future inheritance in "the kingdom of Christ and of God" (4:30; 5:5). They can lose the battle with the powers of evil (6:10-17) and, as disobedient children, experience "God's wrath" (5:6).

The first series of contrasts here deals with the "old self" (Adam) and the "new self" (Christ) (4:17-32).

Paul's picture in this passage of the mind and way of life of the Gentiles is a negative one. "The futility of their thinking," their "darkened . . . understanding," and their "ignorance" relate to their idolatry—the prime Gentile sin to both Jews and Paul. Out of their idolatry come "sensuality" and "every kind of impurity" (4:19).

Specific sins are mentioned. They are social in nature and therefore destructive of unity: lying, resentment, stealing, evil talk, hateful actions, and lust.

"That, however, is not the way of life you learned," Paul explodes in 4:20. *Christ* (Messiah) is synonymous with spiritual and moral transformation. That is why Paul came. Students in his school, where the truth is taught, should know this! His curriculum, as it were, teaches and leads to new creation, in which one becomes like God and lives an upright and holy life (4:24).

What this life is like Paul develops by contrast with the sins he has mentioned. The heart of it is this: loving attitudes and actions, a forgiving spirit, and wholesome, edifying social relationships. The life to which Paul is calling them is summed up in the exhortation, "Follow God's example" (5:1), that is, we should reproduce in our lives what we have seen in Christ and in God!

The second series of contrasts (5:3-20) puts the old "darkness" over against the new "light" and "the disobedient" against the "children of light" (5:6-14). The latter are told not to associate with the former, not to share in their way of life, and to reprove their evil deeds. In spite of the arguments of some, sexually immoral, indecent, and greedy people will have no part in the coming inheritance.

Christians are *saints* (set apart for God) and are to "find out what pleases the Lord" (5:10): sexual purity, chaste speech, magnanimity (not being covetous or greedy), wise use of the time before the end (5:16), sobriety, and Spirit-filled singing and thanksgiving.

■ **Ephesians 5:21–6:9.** The church's responsibility to be and act like "children of light" extends to the homes of its members. Three domestic relationships are addressed in this section: partners in marriage, children and parents, slaves and masters.

Authority and fitting subordination to it were widely emphasized in Paul's world and by him (Romans 13:1-7; 1 Corinthians 11:2-16; 1 Peter 2:13-20). In Ephesians, the principle is applied to wives, children, and slaves as consonant with "reverence for Christ" (5:21). The first Christians were not anarchists or social reformers, though they sowed seeds that later brought about basic social changes (as, for example, in the institution of slavery).

The relationship of husbands and wives is glorified here by comparing it with the relation of Christ and the church.

The subordination of children to Christian parents is supported by an appeal to what is proper to their common relationship to Christ and by an appeal to divine law and promise.

The direction to fathers concerning the benevolent use of authority tempers the absolute power of life and death over children allowed in Roman law.

Christian slaves are to serve their masters as they do Christ—gladly and wholeheartedly—remembering the while that the Lord will reward them for faithful service.

Slave masters are to remember that they have a heavenly Master who will hold them accountable for the way they treat their slaves.

■ **Ephesians 6:10-20.** The church will need strength to live its life and bear its witness in the world. That strength is available through union with the Lord (6:10).

In the battle with superhuman evil powers ("the devil"), the Christian wears God's armor. The Christian has superb defensive and offensive weapons, such as conquering Roman soldiers and the Messiah would wear (Isaiah 11:2-5). Above all, the Christian has intercessory prayer and is part of a fellowship of prayer in which all, including Paul, are supported. The proclamation of the gospel will go forward. Ultimate victory is assured! "The kingdom of Christ and of God" will come!

DIMENSION THREE: WHAT DOES THE BIBLE MEAN TO ME?

Ephesians 4:1-16—Unity in Diversity

Think about the church to which you belong—both the local church and the denomination. What elements are serving to bind the church together at all levels? What forces are fragmenting it at each level? Which of these elements and forces are genuinely "Christian" and which are not, and why? What can be done to eliminate the non-Christian ones?

Ephesians 4:17-5:20—Portrait of a Christian

Paul mentions a lot of things here that the Christian ought not to be and ought to be. Draw together from this section what you consider the most important characteristics of the Christian character and life. Measure yourself by these. Does Paul offer you any help in getting from where you are to where you ought to be?

Ephesians 5:21-23—Christian Marriage

Paul here sets forth the relation of Christ to the church as the founder and model of Christian marriage. He says that this involves the subordination of the wife to the husband and the husband's totally unselfish love of the wife. To what extent, if at all, should this be the model for Christian marriage today? How have the feminist movement of our time and our understanding of human sexuality contributed to the discussion of Christian marriage?

Ephesians 6:10-20—Christian Warfare?

Ephesians is about peace, the peace that God in Christ is bringing to the cosmos through the church (1:2; 2:14, 15,

17; 4:3; 6:15, 23). It seems strange that, as the climax of such writing, the author should introduce a military metaphor and describe the Christian's role as that of a warrior with defensive and offensive weapons.

To what extent do you think the military metaphor accurately characterizes the Christian's situation and task in the world, and in what ways may it obscure it? What truth is Paul trying to convey by the metaphor? How does this truth speak to you in your life situation?

About the Writer

Dr. Edward P. Blair was professor emeritus of New Testament interpretation at Garrett-Evangelical Theological Seminary, Evanston, Illinois.

Printed in the USA
CPSIA information can be obtained
at www.ICGtesting.com
LVHW081651280724
786446LV00009B/241